THE
WINDSOR CHAIR

THOMAS JEFFERSON'S WRITING WINDSOR

Seated in this chair he wrote the first draft of the Declaration of Independence in late June, 1776. Its deviation in design from that of a standard Philadelphia comb-back armchair strongly indicates that he actually designed this chair. It dates 1775 or 1776 and presumably was made to his order by one of the Philadelphia Windsor chairmakers. The American Philosophical Society, Philadelphia, also has in its collection Jefferson's first draft of the Declaration of Independence. Jefferson was president of the Society for eighteen years.

THE
WINDSOR CHAIR

by

THOMAS H. ORMSBEE

DEERFIELD BOOKS, INC.

DISTRIBUTED BY

HEARTHSIDE PRESS, INC., NEW YORK

To
Dr. Meyer Abrahams

Books by Thomas H. Ormsbee

Early American Furniture Makers

The Story of American Furniture

Collecting Antiques in America

Staffordshire Pottery
    (with Josiah Wedgwood)

Antique Furniture of the Walnut Period
    (with R. W. Symonds)

A Storehouse of Antiques

Prime Antiques and Their Current Prices

Care and Repair of Antiques

Field Guide to Early American Furniture

Field Guide to American Victorian Furniture

English China and Its Marks

The Windsor Chair

CONTENTS

INDEX

American Windsor Chairs

English Windsor Chairs

10

ILLUSTRATIONS

Section 1

ORIGIN AND SPREAD OF THE WINDSOR CHAIR

The Windsor chair was of English birth and breeding. During its long span it was as characteristic in a furniture way of English rural life as Cheshire cheese or Toby Philpot himself. Although experts who climb family trees have not traced the Windsor back to 1066 and that mass Norman migration spearheaded by William the Conqueror, its ancestry does reach back to the Gothic period.

Proof of this is to be seen in the massive, three-leg chair, still preserved at St. Cross Hospital in Winchester, which seems to be the only one of its kind that has survived. Here, in design and structure, we see the prototype of the Windsor. From this, and chairs like it, sprang the equally simple but less massive ones which came from the hands of wheelwrights, dating from the sixteenth century or later. Made by these craftsmen principally concerned with shaped spokes, curved felloes and hubs, it was an easy transition. Legs and spindles were shaped by draw-shave as were the spokes. The curved arm was bent much the same as the felloe and in place of the hub, they fashioned, from plank-thick wood, a U-shaped seat with straight front.

The result was a plain sturdy chair of Windsor lines. Known from surviving wheelright chairs of later date, it serves as the connecting link between the Gothic chair and the Windsor made by rural English craftsmen, beginning sometime during the last quarter of the seventeenth century. By the start of the eighteenth century Windsors were well established as simple chairs for use in farmhouses, gardens, taverns

15

and the like. Two of the earliest London mentions of them were an auction notation of 1728 in which lot number 41 included a "Windsor chair" and an advertisement of 1730 by John Brown of St. Paul's Churchyard in which he had for sale "All sorts of Windsor Garden Chairs, of all sizes painted green or in the wood."

How such chairs gained their name has never been substantiated. One account (believed to have originated in America and dating from the early days of collecting) is that George III found such a chair in a farm cottage where he took refuge from a passing shower. Since it was comfortable and suited to his ample bulk he secured others like it for Windsor Castle. This unlikely anecdote does not hold water for "Farmer George" did not ascend the throne until 1760—about a half century after the time when *Windsor* had become the accepted name for chairs of this kind.

Instead, use of the name probably came about in a much less regal way. These chairs were a considerable product of the beech woodlands of Buckinghamshire and, loaded on farm wagons, were peddled throughout the surrounding countryside. One of the logical places to sell them was the town of Windsor with its numerous taverns only fifteen miles distant. From Windsor such chairs could easily reach London, twenty-two miles to the east and connected by a broad highway. There they most likely became identified with Windsor, the market town where they could be bought readily. They at least found favor in London as garden chairs as mentioned in Brown's advertisement.

In addition to Buckinghamshire, Windsors were also made by the rural craftsmen of Suffolk, Lancashire, Yorkshire and other scattering counties. Their production even extended into Wales and Scotland.

By 1750 or soon afterward, Windsors were produced by

various London chairmakers, some of whom embellished them with such refinements as curved cabriole legs instead of the traditional turned ones and replaced some, if not all the spindles with back splats pierced in Gothic and other patterns. Even so, the Windsor never became sufficiently fashionable for plates of it to be included in Chippendale's *Director* or other furniture design manuals. Hence we lack an illustrated case history of this chair. Knowledge of the types made depends on the varying examples that have survived and are now in public or private collections. From study of such chairs we know that the English Windsor, for the most part, remained a sturdy chair of simple lines without much elaboration and was chiefly used by country people or those living in provincial towns.

Just when High Wycombe in Buckinghamshire became an important, if not the chief, center of Windsor chair production has not been completely documented but about 1800 would be a safe date. Once established there, Windsor chairmaking prospered steadily and became family businesses in which sons succeeded fathers, as with the Glenister and Goodchild families. High Wycombe production of Windsors continued throughout most of the nineteenth century, using working ways essentially those of the handcraftsmen instead of factory methods. A few were so made after 1900.

The Windsor held its public far longer than any other chair design. The reasons were obvious. It was strong enough to survive hard daily use through the years. Because of its compact, functional structure it handled easily and lent itself readily to any setting other than that of a sophisticated formal room. Its moderate cost put it within the reach of people of average means and its upkeep called for nothing more than an occasional repainting.

All these points in its favor highly commended the Windsor

to potential chair buyers in both England and America for a span of close to a century and a half. This was particularly true of American Windsors. Here from about 1730 to 1870 they were made in greater volume and variety than any other type of chair. During these years American craftsmen, many of whom specialized as Windsor chairmakers, made them in nine distinct designs. Nor did they stop there. From their hands also came high chairs and those of small size for children, writing chairs with broad tablet arm, turned-leg Windsor tables and now and then a Windsor cradle.

Although native to England it was in America that the Windsor developed that grace of line that converted it from a common farmhouse or tavern piece to one not out of place in handsome colonial homes of the day. It was in America that the Windsor chair, popular with affluent families as well as with sturdy farmers and economy-minded tavern keepers, came into its own.

Quite possibly the place where it first appeared had something to do with this, since it was Philadelphia, already beginning to be known as the London of the New World. Here in 1708 one finds an inventory of a John Jones, merchant, who died possessed of a Windsor chair. This was probably of English origin for actual American Windsor chairmaking at the earliest did not begin before 1725. Indeed the first of them were probably made either by chairmakers who had migrated there recently or were produced by Philadelphia craftsmen who had seen imported examples and set about adapting the Windsor idea to American tastes. The result was a chair with more splay to the legs than the English importations. Into the U-shaped top rail of the low back were fitted ten to twelve tapering spindles instead of the usual ornamental back splat and spindles. Further, being made by urban artisans, these Philadelphia chairs, as they were called at first, took on

18

a nicety of line and detail lacking in the provincial chair from which they sprang.

Under their hands the chair of the English cottager developed into a piece suited to the residence of a country squire or similar worthy. Even handsome town houses were not entirely without one or more of them. Although these Windsors with an American accent made their debut in Philadelphia as low-back and comb-back chairs, there was such intrenched opposition from makers of rush-bottomed turned chairs that some years went by before they gained a dominant position.

By about 1740 Windsor chair production was by way of becoming a specialized craft, though sometimes combined with that of rush-bottom chairmaking. Philadelphia makers at this time included John Brientnall who died in 1747; Francis Trumble, for many years a prolific maker of Windsors who started working about 1740; Thomas Ackley, with his shop on Fourth Street near Market, who had been apprenticed to Solomon Fussell, rush-bottom chairmaker and son-in-law of John Brientnall; Josiah Sherald who was still making Windsors and rush-bottom chairs in 1760 and Richmonde, first name unknown, who was one of the first Philadelphia craftsmen to become a Windsor specialist. Meanwhile Windsor chair production had begun to spread to other colonies—New Jersey where at New Brunswick there was Richard Jacques who from about 1750 made both Windsors and spinning wheels, a logical combination since both called for nicely turned parts.

In New York there was Andrew Gautier as shown by his advertising which appeared in the *New York Gazette* for April 18, 1765. This, as far as is known, was the first time in America that a picture of a Windsor chair was published. His advertisement, illustrated with a crudely done woodcut of a comb-back Windsor, reads:

"To be sold

By ANDREW GAUTIER

In Prince-Street

Opposite Mr. David Provost's near Broad-Street

A Large and neat Assortment of Windsor Chairs, made in the best and neatest Manner, and well painted, VIZ. Highback's, low back's and Sackback's Chairs and Settees, or double seated fit for Piazza or Gardens. . . . . Children's dining and low Chairs & c.

N.B. As the above GAUTIER intends constantly to keep a large Number of all Sorts of the above Chairs by him for Sale, all persons wanting such, may depend on being supplied with any Quantity Wholesale or Retail at Reasonable Rates."

Whether Gautier was a former Philadelphia apprentice is not known but his illustrated advertisement throws much light on Windsors of that time since it is specific as to the types in use and includes what I believe to be the first known mention of Windsors made especially for children.

Prior to the American Revolution Windsor chairs were well known in most of the other colonies. In part this was the result of the many of Philadelphia make carried to various seaport towns along the Atlantic coast. An instance of this is this Charleston, South Carolina advertisement which appeared in the *South Carolina Gazette* on June 23, 1766.

"Imported from Philadelphia in the Brigantine Philadelphia Packet, Francis Johnson, Master, and to be sold by Sheed & White at their store in Church Street. A large and neat assortment of Windsor Chairs, made in the best and neatest manner, well painted, high back'd, low back'd, sack back's and settees or double seated, fit for piazzas or gardens, childrens dining and low chairs."

20

At the same time that shippers were sending chairs to the other colonies and even to the West Indies, craftsmen who had learned Windsor chairmaking in Philadelphia were migrating to greener pastures and stressing their Philadelphia training. John Kelso was one of these. In the *New York Gazette and Weekly Mercury* of August 8, 1774, he advertised:

> "John Kelso, Windsor Chair-Maker, from Philadelphia, at Mr. Hyer's in Broad Street, next door to the General's Makes and sells all kinds of Windsor chairs . . . . ., on the most remarkable terms; and as he served a regular apprenticeship in one of the first shops in that way in Philadelphia, he is persuaded he can supply those who may be kind enough to favour him with their custom, with as well-finish'd, strong and neat work as ever appeared in this city."

By or before 1770 Windsor chairmaking was a recognized trade in the New England colonies, notably Massachusetts, Connecticut and Rhode Island. Once this trade gained a foothold there it prospered in one form or another for some seventy-five years. Among the eighteenth century New England Windsor chairmakers there were Alpheus Hews, New Haven, Connecticut; Daniel Lawrence, Providence, Rhode Island; Luther Metcalf, Medway, Massachusetts; Elisha Richardson, Franklin, Massachusetts; Stacy Stackhouse, Hartford, Connecticut; Ebenezer Stone, Boston, Massachusetts and Colonel Ebenezer Tracy, Lisbon, Connecticut, best known of all the Connecticut makers of Windsors.

With the beginning of the nineteenth century, making Windsors was being widely done in all of the older sections of the country and had even migrated westward into Kentucky where James Hardwick and Isaac Holmes were well established before 1810 in Lexington.

About 1820 the demand for Sheraton painted fancy chairs was large enough so that a good many Windsor craftsmen added these other chairs to their line and began advertising that they made both kinds. For instance John K. Cowperthwaite of New York City used an elaborate billhead with a picture of his establishment at 4 Chatham Square designating it as "Fancy & Windsor Chair Manufactory."

Windsors continued to be made in an increasing number of cities and towns until about 1850 when factory-made products crowded them out. One of the early types of factory-produced chairs was a revival of the low-back Windsor of the mid-eighteenth century, in a debased form, the kind that has come to be known as the Firehouse Windsor. This in turn was the forerunner of even a later chair of the Windsor type, the captain's chair which has now become collectible as a semi-antique.

Section II

AMERICAN WINDSOR CRAFTSMANSHIP

From the beginning the American Windsor was a specialized chair. Its development speaks loudly of the skill and originality of the craftsmen who so styled themselves. These men had no books of design to which they could turn for suggestions. They proceeded unassisted save for a few Windsors brought from England, recollections of rural Buckinghamshire chairs or more elaborate ones from the hands of London-trained craftsmen who had migrated to Philadelphia.

Consequently American Windsors soon developed their own characteristics. These were both structural and decorative. American-made Windsors are outstanding because each part is adequate in size and strength for its purpose but never made larger than its structural requirement, be it leg, stretcher, seat, arm or spindle.

Likewise, skill of design and thoroughness of workmanship were such that even today, there are many, many Windsors strong and sound as when new. Legs and spindles were so firmly seated that they are still tightly in place. This test of time speaks volumes for the sound work of the men who made these chairs, especially when it is remembered that the Windsor was originally for masculine use and hard wear in meeting place, tavern or home. Practically never does one find a Windsor that is loose in its joints unless it has met with an accident and been imperfectly repaired, something that cannot be said for cabinet-makers' chairs of the same vintage.

Since they bought their supply of wood in the form of roughly finished planks and the like, these Windsor craftsmen

25

had to be proficient in several branches of wood working. To make legs, spindles and other turned parts, they must be good turners, well versed in the intricacies of working on a lathe with an assortment of turner's chisels and skilled enough to produce multiple parts with exactly the same detail. To produce bows, continuous arms and other bent parts they must be skilled at steaming and bending. Such parts they shaped with the aid of frames where the hot pliable parts were pegged until dry and permanently bent to the desired shape, whether it be a simple curved bow or a more elaborate one intended for an arch-back chair. Bending was also required for the comb-pieces with their concave curve and for bent arm supports sometimes used instead of baluster turned spindles.

There was the task of shaping the seats for which the raw material was ample blocks cut from two-inch thick plank. First they had to be given the desired outline, whether shield-shaped or elliptical. After that came "dishing," that is, cutting away the upper surface to make it body conforming. Sometimes this could be as much as half the thickness of the seat. Even working with knotless pine or whitewood, finishing a seat so that it was exactly symmetrical with its central pommel and curved edge called for nicety of work and a keen eye. Further, a Windsor craftsman must be a skillful carver to accomplish knuckle carving on the ends of the continuous arm and the volutes with which the ears of some comb-pieces were finished. Lastly when the Windsors were completed he must be ready to paint them as the customer desired.

Contributing materially to design and execution of American Windsors was the variety of native woods available. All were bountiful and, as any of these craftsmen would have expressed it, "worked well." The standard woods were pine, whitewood, chestnut, maple, white oak, hickory and ash. Each was used for a specific part or parts according to the section where a particular craftsman worked. The plank-thick seats were consistently fashioned of knot-free pine or whitewood or, sometimes in Connecticut, chestnut. These soft woods had the advantage of being easy to shape and the merit of being free from any tendency to warp or split as they aged.

Maple was used for legs, stretchers and arm stumps since it was close grained and could be readily shaped with lathe and cutting chisels. It also formed the heavy continuous arm of the low-back chair. Maple was used too for fashioning the flat splats of arrow-back chairs. Whether hand-shaped as was done at first or lathe-turned which came later, hickory was the favorite spindle wood although white oak and ash were sometimes used.

These three woods were preferred material for the loops of loop-back chairs, for the bow of bow-backs and the intricately shaped top rail of the arch-back since they did not fracture during the process of steaming and bending. Another part shaped by steaming and bending, the comb-piece, was apt to be of hickory or white oak with ash used less often because of its tendency to splinter when cut so thin.

Such was the assortment of woods used most frequently by Windsor craftsmen but this selection did not always hold, especially with workmen who followed the well-tried economy rule of "use it up, make it do, do without" and took whatever woods happened to be at hand as substitutes for the usual material. Since Windsor chairs were painted in solid colors, green, black, red, white and sometimes brown, it was unimportant what woods were concealed beneath. So, today in the process of refinishing, an occasional Windsor can be found with substitutions of woods that are in the nature of exceptions.

Just as the woods used varied, assembling of Windsors differed to suit the working ways of the individual craftsman.

27

Some did it one way and others slightly differently. The thick plank seat as a practical way was the starting point for assembling an individual chair by addition of the turned and shaped parts that would become legs, stretchers, arm and back. This assembly called for very neat and exact work and in doing it the Windsor workers must have had a more or less standard method of procedure but what this was we can only hazard the guess that it started with attaching the legs on which the chair would stand firmly and solidly. In doing this, some craftsmen used unseasoned wood for both seat and legs knowing that when these parts dried the natural shrinkage would result in joints that were vise-tight. Others used thoroughly dried and seasoned wood.

In making a Windsor chair the first step was shaping of the seat and hollowing out the upper surface to be body conforming or saddled. In outline these seats were of varying degrees of shield shape except for the oval-shaped seat of the typical New England bow-back chair. There were some four variations of the shield shape. There was the U-shape seat with nearly straight front of the early low-back and comb-back chairs, mostly of Philadelphia or New York provenance; the more pronounced shield shape with bowed front and scrolled sides characteristic of the loop-back, fan-back and arch-back chairs; approximately the same shape with a tail-piece at the rear, used for brace-back chairs, and the squarish shield shape, most often found with rod-back and the later arrow-back chairs.

The upper surface of all seats had a well-rounded edge at the front which met with an upward curve from the underside of the seat. Saddle shaping of the upper surface to make it body conforming, with its central pommel simply or boldly done, was sometimes so pronounced that the thickness of the seat at center had been reduced by half. This was of course accomplished with adzes and gouging chisels, followed by smoothing with block planes.

After the seat had been shaped from a piece of plank about two inches thick, attaching the legs and stretchers followed. There were two ways of applying the legs. They could be inserted into holes that penetrated the seat, as with a good many chairs both early and late. When this was done, legs were made fast by downward driven wedges and presumably liberal use of glue. With the second method, the leg holes did not penetrate the seat but were bored only three-quarters of the seat thickness and had a slight reverse flare. A blind or fox wedge was then inserted in each leg and when this was driven home the leg end was expanded enough to make a firm and tightly glued joint. This was so well accomplished that today it is almost impossible to remove a leg so set in place without damaging the socket end.

Incidentally, boring the holes called for careful workmanship. First they must be far enough in from the edge of the seat lest it split when the legs were in place. Early chairs had these holes three or four inches inside the perimeter of the seat. More important still was the angle of boring since it determined the flare or rake of the legs. This bold flare was a characteristic of American Windsors from the start and continued until the advent of the fire-house type. The splay angle varied from ten to 15 degrees from the perpendicular with the sidewise flare often more noticeable than that at front or back.

Leg turnings were done on the foot treadle lathes then in use and accomplished with such nicety that all four legs of a given chair matched exactly. Turnings also had distinct regional variations: (1) blunt-arrow with ball or ball-and-ring foot, found on chairs of early Philadelphia or New York provenance; (2) long, slender tapering foot surmounted by simple baluster turning, found on chairs of general New England origin; (3) tapering foot, incurved for Rhode Island and (4) a shorter and less slender tapered foot surmounted by baluster turning of greater diameter, particular to chairs of Connecticut make.

Toward the close of the eighteenth century these distinctively turned legs were replaced either by those with bobbin shaping or by slenderer ones with slight ring turnings that simulated bamboo. Legs of this sort were used on chairs of all sections, sometimes contemporary with regional types.

American Windsors were consistently braced by the H-shape recessed stretcher. Designs of these lathe-turned parts included ring-and-ball, ring-and-bobbin and plain bobbin. They were so placed that the greatest diameter was where the ends of the central recessed member were socketed into the side members. Holes bored by these socket joints did not penetrate and the joints were made fast by blind wedging and glue or with glue only. Stretchers were turned of seasoned wood with ends given a slight hollow groove. When driven into their sockets, the shrinkage that came with further drying resulted in joints that would not loosen even with the hard usage that was the lot of many Windsors.

With earlier chairs, the seat was 18 inches from the floor. Later ones measured from 16½ to 17 inches. This rule holds except for a chair especially made for an unusually small person. Here all dimensions would be slightly reduced with seat 14½ or 15 inches from the floor. Except for one of these rarities (Nutting in his long experience is credited with recording but one such example where a Windsor seat is less than 16½ inches high) a low seat is certain evidence that at some time in the past its legs were shortened for one reason or another, of which converting to a rocking chair was the most common. Save for an occasional rod-back, and I have heard of only one example, the first of the Windsor family

30

to have been made originally as a rocker was the arrow-back. Earlier ones were altered during the rocking chair era.

So much for the construction of the Windsor underbody. This completed, the chair was ready for its upper structure. Forming the arm and back was done by anchoring the lower ends of all members into sockets bored in the seat. For this discussion of construction the back can be said to consist of an arm and outer members with the area which these surround provided with from three to nine spindles.

With all Windsors, whether side or armchair, shaping and construction of the back determined its type from low-back through the nine variations that give each its name. With an armchair the back consisted of a continuous arm supported at its outer ends by turned or shaped arm supports. The area so framed was filled with nicely spaced spindles varying in number. Arm supports were socketed into holes that penetrated the seat but not so with the spindles. Their lower ends were held in place by holes bored only part way through the seat.

The same was true of the upper ends which were inserted in partially bored holes in the top rail, be it the heavy continuous arm of the low-back chair, the wide comb of a comb-back and so on through the bow-back, fan-back and arch-back types. These socket joints were mostly blind-wedged and glued. With both the comb-back and bow-back, the spindles also passed through holes bored in the shaped continuous arm.

In the rod-back type the upper ends of the spindles were either set by blind wedging and glue on partially bored holes of the top turned member or they penetrated it. Shaping the spindles was delicate work. Earlier ones were less slender, about three-quarters of an inch in diameter, because they were rounded by use of knives and draw-shaves. Sometimes they have a bobbin-like bulge toward the lower end that can be

31

quite pronounced with some examples. Spindles with this bulge, mostly found on early bow-back chairs, have the enlargement below the middle as a long slender taper was required further up to pass through the holes bored in the continuous arm. It not only indicated handwork but gave a decorative effect.

A little later spindles were lathe-turned. This was accomplished by use of an added ring support for the revolving spindle. This turning of slender tapering spindles called for considerable skill on the part of the turner as they varied in length. Those of a comb-back armchair were sometimes as much as 42 or 44 inches long and those of bow-back chairs ranged from about 20 to 28 inches in length. Tapering and from three-quarters to half an inch in diameter, their turning on a fast revolving lathe required a skilled and alert operator to counteract any off center "whipping" during the process. It explains the use of hickory, white oak and ash as favored woods for spindles since they handled better on the lathe than other woods.

With the low-back, its semi-circular arm, usually of maple, was shaped by sawing in two parts and reinforced at the center of the back with a second piece glued in place which formed a cresting. The continuous arm of the comb-back and bow-back chairs was steamed and bent to desired shape and bored for holes through which the tapering spindles passed. Arm ends were finished with a curving flare or were knuckle-carved. Arm supports were usually baluster turned and set with an upward flare.

For the loop-back chair, sometimes known as a balloon-back if the lower ends of the loop were given an inward curve, the shaped loop was anchored in holes that penetrated the seat. The spindles which it framed were socketed in the usual manner. Made both as side and armchair, the latter was provided with cyma-curved arms tenon-joined to the loop and supported at front by baluster or plain turned supports.

The arch-back chair represents one of the neatest feats in bending of any Windsor. Its back, generally fitted with nine tapering spindles, was framed by a one-piece arched hoop with ends bent to form short flat arms. The upper ends of the spindles were of course socketed into the arched hoop and the short arms were supported by baluster-turned stumps, usually sloping forward from seat to arm.

The fan-back chair marks a distinct change in the outline of the earlier Windsors. Its back with slight backward slant was formed by two slender baluster-turned uprights surmounted by a full-width concave yoke-shaped crest rail with either plain or volute carved ends. Between these uprights were from seven to nine equally spaced tapering spindles flaring slightly from seat to crest rail. These spindles were sometimes enhanced with an element of baluster turning. Arms when present were either flat with outward curve terminating in knuckle-carved hand grips or were rectangular cross sections with cyma curved shaping sloping downward from the back. Short baluster-turned members served as supports which were socketed into the seat so as to flare slightly outward. Inner ends of arms were fastened to the back uprights with tenon joints. Between these and the arm supports there were usually two or three short plain spindles.

For additional structural strength the tapering spindle backs of three types of Windsors were reinforced by a pair of flaring bracing spindles. Such construction was done with fan-back, arch-back and loop-back chairs. Here the seats were shaped with a rear tailpiece into which the ends of the bracing spindles were firmly socketed into the bow of the back or the yoke-shaped member that formed the crest rail.

With rod-back chairs, made either as side or armchairs, the

construction was somewhat simplified. The back was outlined by two uprights turned somewhat larger than the spindles and the cresting was accomplished either by a turned cross member or a shaped top rail. The uprights were anchored in socket holes that penetrated the seat and their upper ends were fixed in sockets if the crest piece was turned or by tenon joints if shaped. Arms when present were made of turned parts the same size as the uprights which resulted in slightly flaring arms of remarkable strength considering that they were turned members. Space below the arms was fitted with one to four spindles matching those of the back. Not only were the turned parts of rod-back chairs made lighter than those of earlier Windsors but this lightness was accentuated by the use of bamboo ring turnings which added to the decorative effect as a whole.

Plan of construction of arrow-back Windsors which came about 1810, broke sharply with that of the preceding rod-backs. The supporting uprights were now given a reverse curve, flattened on the front and surmounted by a flat, slightly concave crest rail. Instead of slender tapering spindles there were from three to five arrow-shaped splats, a feature that gave this type of Windsor its name. When made with arms, these were shaped rectangles joined to the back uprights by tenon joints and finished with rolled ends. With some of the rocker armchairs the crest rail was surmounted by a headrest in the form of a flat comb-piece supported by spindles. Where earlier chairs were painted in a single color, arrow-backs were enhanced by stenciling on crest rail and splats done in color and parcel gilding. This reflected the Sheraton fancy chairs then being produced in large numbers and resulted in a more colorful chair than any of the earlier Windsors.

The comb-piece or headrest which sometimes appeared on the various types of Windsors, with the exception of the fan-back, called for considerable skill in its making. It began with

34

steaming and bending. The latter was done with clamps and a form to produce the proper degree of concave curve. Then it was shaped and in so doing the upper edge was thinned almost to knife-edge sharpness and the lower one was never more than half or five-eighths of an inch thick. Boring holes for the spindles that would be fitted into it called for extra fine workmanship. For a final touch with some comb-pieces the ears were enhanced by delicately carved volutes. All this explains why comb-back Windsors have a style that makes them among the most desired of the entire Windsor family.

The writing Windsor which originated in America and was an unknown kind as far as the English makers were concerned, presented several construction problems. The seat could not be made symmetrical because of the extension needed on the right side for the two to four turned members that were socketed into the seat to support the writing arm or tablet. This in turn was attached to the upper side of the continuous arm firmly or, less frequently, by a pivot so that the tablet rotated enough to bring it to the most convenient position for the user. A small box-like drawer for writing materials was attached under the arm and sometimes a second drawer was under the seat. Obviously the extra work made these writing Windsors more expensive and probably explains why fewer were made. However, they were made in all the variations, even the late firehouse Windsor.

Whether a writing Windsor was ever made to suit the whim of somebody who was left handed has long been a moot question, even with Windsor chair enthusiasts but I can now state that they were made. In the collection of the Henry Ford Museum at Dearborn there is a left-handed writing Windsor. It is of the rod-back type and dates about 1825. It is illustrated with other writing Windsors in Section III (see Illustration 42). Undoubtedly far fewer left-handed chairs were produced than those for right-handed people. After all the old Windsor craftsmen worked in an era where a left-handed member of a family was not humored in his aberration but forcibly corrected.

The Windsor settee presented no special construction problem. It varied in size from the love-seat to one seating four or five people. The rectangular plank seat had a straight front, made with some degree of saddling that determined its kind. Windsor settees were made in the low-back, comb-back, bow-back, arch-back and rod-back types. Love-seats were made with four legs; larger ones had six, eight, ten and even twelve, well-braced with recessed stretchers having ball-and-ring or bobbin turnings. The low-back settee sometimes had as many as 38 baluster or simply turned spindles. These low-backs are more numerous than other types. Comb-backs are unusual, not to say rare. The tall spindles are surmounted by a comb-piece with or without ears and the continuous arm is crested and terminates with nice volutes. Bow-back settees were usually made with a single elongated bow but some fine examples were produced with overlapping triple bows.

Section III

NINE TYPES OF
AMERICAN WINDSOR CHAIRS
AND RELATED PIECES

EARLY LOW-BACK WINDSOR ARMCHAIR

Chairs like this one were probably the first type of American Windsors. They are considered to have been made first in Philadelphia about 1740. Others like them were produced in New Jersey and New York as late as 1780 but apparently not in New England.

Distinctive features are (1) continuous curved arm with applied cresting at back and terminating in out-curved ends; (2) outer baluster spindles boldly turned and as many as seventeen plain spindles; (3) U-shaped saddle seat with straight front and central pommel and (4) well splayed turned legs of the blunt-arrow type braced by a recessed stretcher with bulbous turning.

38

Illustration 2   *—Alfred Arnold*

LATER LOW-BACK WINDSOR ARMCHAIR

Chairs with these details date ca. 1750–1780. Made in New Jersey, New York and Pennsylvania, their distinguishing features are (1) taller shaping of the central cresting for the continuous arm; (2) back has thirteen plain spindles spaced a little wider apart than those in earlier chair and (3) baluster-turned instead of blunt-arrow legs, braced by a recessed stretcher of slightly lighter bulbous turning.

40

Illustration 3   *—Ginsburg & Levy, Inc.*

PHILADELPHIA COMB-BACK ARMCHAIR, CA. 1760

About the same time as the low-back chairs, Philadelphia craftsmen also produced the more imposing comb-back armchair. A development of the low-back, it had the definite advantage of a taller back in giving ease and support to the human frame. Comb-back chairs date about 1750 to 1780. They were first made in Philadelphia and eastern Pennsylvania. Others were produced later in New Jersey, New York and New England.

The conforming back is formed by from five to nine spindles. These continue through the horseshoe-shaped arm and are surmounted by a yoke-shaped crest rail similar in outline to that of the ornamental comb worn by women of the period. It can have either plain ends or volute-carved ears. The sides of the continuous arm are supported by three short spindles and the ends by baluster-turned arm stumps. The saddle seat is U-shaped with straight front and central pommel. The flaring turned legs are of the blunt-arrow type and are braced by an H-shaped recessed stretcher with plain bulbous or ring and bulbous turning.

42

Illustration 4   *—Israel Sack, Inc.*

NEW ENGLAND COMB-BACK ARMCHAIR

The chief difference between comb-back armchairs of New England origin and those of Pennsylvania, New Jersey and New York was use of baluster-turned legs, often with marked vase shaping, like those of this chair. Here also the back is unusually tall, being forty-two inches from seat to comb-piece which has plain uncarved ends.

44

Illustration 5

COMB-BACK ARMCHAIR WITH SERPENTINE
SUPPORTS

Clearly of Pennsylvania provenance, this chair which dates about 1760, has serpentine arm supports instead of the more usual baluster-turned outer spindles. The continuous arm is thicker because of the applied cresting through which pass the seven plain spindles of the slightly flaring back. The surmounting comb-piece has swirl-carved ends. Instead of a U-shaped saddle seat, this one is shield-shaped. The supporting legs are of the blunt-arrow type modified with ring turnings and the recessed stretcher is bulbous, flanked by rings. Width of seat is about quarter less than those of the two preceding chairs.

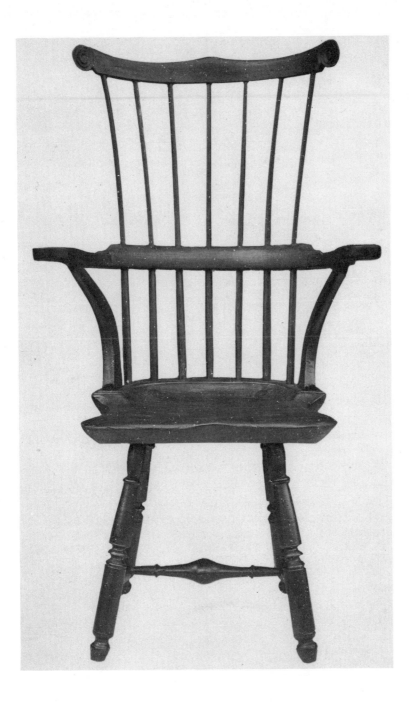

Illustration 6   *—Ginsburg & Levy, Inc.*

NEW ENGLAND COMB-BACK WITH
SHAPED SPINDLES

Of New England provenance and dating about 1760 before spindles were lathe-turned, this chair is of more delicate proportions than the Philadelphia examples. Its comb-piece is well shaped with accentuated ears that are uncarved. The back is formed by seven spindles with bobbin shaping below the continuous bent arm. The ends are supported by slender baluster turned supports with distinct outward flare. The shield-shaped seat does not have deeply cut saddling, the sides have bold cyma curves and the front edge is slightly rounded. The baluster-turned legs, set with a pronounced rake, have bold vase shaping and tall tapering feet. Length of leg and correspondingly high seat are unusual, suggesting that this chair was made for desk use or possibly for the presiding officer of a meeting.

48

Illustration 7

UNUSUAL NEW ENGLAND COMB-BACK CHAIR

Probably made by a country craftsman, this chair does not follow the pattern of other comb-backs in its lines and construction. It has a two-story back composed of seven tall spindles which pass through the continuous arm, through a flat crest rail and terminate in a wide slightly oval shaped comb-piece. From the crest rail to the level of the bent continuous arm, these spindles are flanked by ram's horn outer members which support the crest rail. All of the spindles have a slight bobbin shaping below the arm. The ends of the arm which are slightly rounded are supported by simply turned outer spindles. The seat is oval in shape with little or no saddling. Legs have a slight bamboo turning. The recessed stretcher is bulbous-turned. Design of this chair can best be considered a cross-breed, mostly Windsor with some attributes of the Sheraton fancy chair. It probably dates between 1810 and 1815. The rockers are a later edition.

50

Illustration 8

—L. T. Hunt

EARLY BOW-BACK ARMCHAIR

The bow-back or "sack-back" chair, as it was called by the men who produced it, was made by both English and American Windsor chairmakers. It made its appearance on the American scene in Philadelphia about 1750 or 1760. It proved one of the most popular of the Windsor types and during the ensuing years was made by craftsmen of all sections for about seventy-five years. Hence more bow-back Windsors are still available today than any other type dating back that far.

This first form of the bow-back with blunt-arrow legs is the rarest. It has a continuous crested arm with knuckle-carved ends which is surmounted by a well-sprung symmetrically bent bow. The back is formed by nine plain spindles that pass through the arm and are socketed into the surmounting bow. The seat is a modified U-shape with some saddling. Legs are braced by an H-shaped stretcher with bulbous or bulbous-and-ring turning.

52

Illustration 9   —*John K. Byard*

NEW ENGLAND EIGHTEENTH CENTURY
BOW-BACK WINDSORS

The bow-back found ready acceptance in all parts of New England, especially Massachusetts, Rhode Island and Connecticut. It was made by craftsmen of this section in considerable quantity with both seven and nine spindle backs. To illustrate this, a chair of each kind is pictured. With both, the continuous arm through which the shaped spindles pass is light and nicely bent. Both terminate with flat rounded ends that are supported by vase-shaped outer spindles that flare forward. The seat, as with almost all bow-back chairs, is oval in outline, saddled with slight pommel shaping. Both chairs have well splayed, baluster-turned legs. Those of the seven spindle back chair are characteristic of Connecticut work. The legs of the nine-spindle example are of the Massachusetts type.

54

CUT-ARM BOW-BACK WINDSOR

Here is an unusual variation of the bow-back chair. Instead of the usual continuous arm with spindles passing through it, there are two short flat arms and the seven tapering spindles rise directly to the bow. The objective was probably a more comfortable chair which was easier to make because of elimination of the bent continuous arm. The short arms are supported by baluster-turned outer spindles and two plain short spindles. This cut-arm Windsor has the same oval-shaped, somewhat saddled seat. Legs, set with medium cant, are of the New England type and fitted with an H-shaped stretcher of bulbous turning. It was made sometime during the last two decades of the eighteenth century. Also the design lacks the symmetry of other bow-back chairs.

Illustration 11   *—Israel Sack, Inc.*

BOW-BACK WINDSOR WITH COMB-PIECE

This is the most imposing of all the chairs of bow-back design. It was accomplished by having the seven tapering spindles of the back pass through not only the continuous arm but also the bow and surmounting the whole with a wide yoke-shaped comb-piece. The latter has a slight concave curve and pronounced up-curved ends or ears. Except for the comb which gives this chair what has been called a triple back, it retains the standard lines of bow-back chairs of the late eighteenth century. It is of New England provenance and leg turnings indicate it was probably made in Connecticut. Although not branded, it could well have come from the hands of John Wadsworth or other Windsor chairmakers working in or near Hartford.

Illustration 12   —Author's Collection

LATE NEW ENGLAND BOW-BACK WINDSOR

Known to have been made near Claremont, New Hampshire about 1825, this chair is typical of country workmanship during the first quarter of the nineteenth century. It is a simple chair with a seven-spindle back. The bent bow is of average height. The continuous arm is thicker than some earlier examples and the ends have simple knuckle carving. It has the usual oval saddled seat. The legs which lack uniform flare, noticeably with the front right, one have simple vase shaping and are fitted with a recessed stretcher that is bulbous-turned. The slight added thickness of the bow at the third and fifth spindles are a repair of many years standing where raw-hide leather was wrapped around a break in the bow at one point and repeated at the other spindle to make it balance.

Illustration 13   *—Ginsburg & Levy, Inc.*

FAN-BACK ARMCHAIR

The design feature that gives this chair its name is a flaring fan-like back, surmounted by a concave serpentine-shaped crest rail with swirl-carved volutes. This is supported by two baluster turned uprights or stiles framing five tapering spindles. The out-curved arms are tenon-joined to the uprights and supported by plain spindles and baluster turned arm stumps. Knuckle carving decorates the arm ends. The seat is elliptical with medium saddling. The baluster-turned legs are of the New England type and are braced by an H-shaped stretcher.

Fan-back chairs were the first to be made in smaller proportions for feminine use but were also produced full size, like the chair illustrated which probably dates about 1770. The fan-back was made in all sections from 1760 to as late as 1800.

62

Illustration 14   *Mildred & Herbert Kaufmann*

FAN-BACK SIDE CHAIR

Fan-back side chairs matched similar armchairs and were probably made in sets for dining room use. Except for arms, they had the same structural features as the armchairs. The back was formed by from five to seven plain or bulbous spindles and the saddled seat was usually shield-shaped.

The chair pictured is of New England provenance. It dates about 1770 and bears the brand of "B. Green," an eighteenth century craftsman of whom there is no record save a few chairs branded with his name.

Illustration 15   *—The H. F. Du Pont Winterthur Museum*

FAN-BACK ARMCHAIR WITH BRACED BACK

Structurally the weakness of the fan-back was its tall and sloping back. Consequently a good proportion of such chairs were provided with a pair of bracing spindles which were anchored in sockets bored in an integral part of the seat at the rear known as a tailpiece. From there the bracing spindles, usually plain and tapering, flared upward to join the crest rail into which they were socketed just inside the outer spindles of the back. They not only added strength but were always so placed as not to interfere with the grace and lines of the fan-back design.

This is apparent in the chair shown here which is an example of fine New England work dating between 1765 and 1770.

Illustration 16   *—John S. Walton, Inc.*

FAN-BACK SIDE CHAIR WITH BRACED BACK

Originally one of a set produced to match an armchair with like structural and decorative details, this side chair is typical of the work of New England Windsor chairmakers in the eighteenth century. The individuality of the maker is shown, however in the arched rather than serpentine crest rail. Also the saddled shield-shaped seat has a more prominent pommel than is usual with chairs of this kind.

68

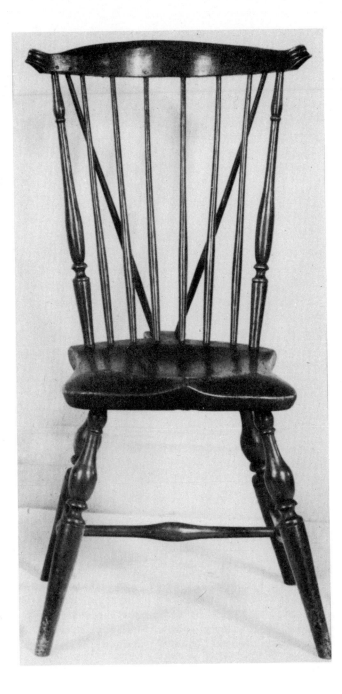

Illustration 17   *—Ruth & Roger Bacon*

FAN-BACK WINDSOR WITH ROUND SEAT

This armchair is an unusual example of the fan-back type because of the circular saddled seat. It also has flat, cyma-curved arms with rounded outer ends. Since the vase turned legs of New England type are not tapered at the lower ends, as is usual, it has been held that the rockers are original and not a later addition. If so, it is an example of a very early Windsor rocking chair.

70

Illustration 18   *—Israel Sack, Inc.*

ARCH-BACK WINDSOR ARMCHAIR

Shaping of the one-piece combination of crest rail and arms shows how skilfully the Windsor chairmakers worked. To produce a broad bow and short flat arms all in one piece, called for both skill and use of a special frame to which the pliable steamed wood was clamped until thoroughly dry. The result can be seen in the example shown here. The arched crest rail surmounts nine long tapering spindles flanked on either side by shorter ones. The outer ends of the arms are supported by larger baluster-turned spindles so placed that they have an outward flare. The saddled seat is shield-shaped and below are the usual vase-shaped turned legs.

The chairs illustrated have the concave tapered foot characteristic of Windsors made in Rhode Island. Arch-back Windsors, as far as is known were made only in New England and date from about 1785 to 1810. As such they represent a high point in this craft.

72

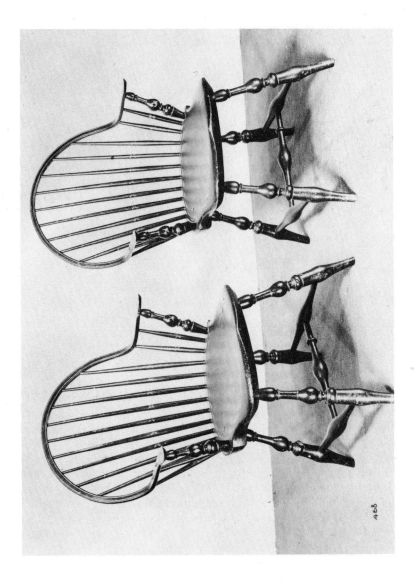

468

Illustration 19

ARCH-BACK ARMCHAIR WITH BRACED BACK

Like the fan-back, some of the arch-back chairs were strengthened by two additional spindles anchored in the tailpiece of the seat and extending at a wide angle to the bow-shaped rail. In the chair illustrated, which dates in the late eighteenth century, the outer vase-shaped spindles that support the arms are set further back and have a more pronounced forward and outward angle than is found in many chairs of this type. The saddled seat is shield-shaped with a nice curving edge and a central pommel. Legs are of the double bobbin-turned kind. As usual, they are braced by a recessed H-shaped stretcher of bulbous turned parts.

74

ARCH-BACK CHAIR WITH COMB-PIECE

Chairs with this elaboration are not as numerous as the standard arch-back without comb. Here the sloping back is surmounted by a flat serpentine comb-piece supported by five tall spindles that pass through the combination one piece crest rail and arms. The result is a taller back (fifty inches) than with most chairs of this kind. It is formed by a boldly U-shaped bow with five long tapering spindles and four shorter ones. The flat short arms end in simple knuckle carving. The seat is oval. The flaring legs are typically New England in their vase-shaped turning and are braced by the standard H-shaped recessed stretcher made of bulbously turned parts. This is a fine chair of late eighteenth century New England provenance.

Some arch-back Windsors with surmounting comb-piece were provided with spindle braces arranged in the same manner as the armchair in Illustration 19 (see).

76

Illustration 21   *—B. Greenberg*

LOOP-BACK ARMCHAIR

Of the late eighteenth century Windsors, those with loop back, originally known as "oval back," were made in larger numbers. Produced as both arm and side chairs, they were the simplest type of Windsors. All had a U-shaped bow with ends socketed into the seat.

The chair illustrated has a nine spindle back with spindles slightly bamboo ringed. The short arms, which are of mahogany and tenon-joined to the bow, have a slight downward cyma curve and terminate in rolled ends. The seat is a modified shield shape. Legs have double bobbin turnings that are bamboo ringed. This chair is branded "G. Gaw," one of the better known Philadelphia chairmakers who worked about 1790.

78

Illustration 22   *—Israel Sack, Inc.*

LOOP-BACK SIDE CHAIR

This chair was the simplest and most easily handled of the eighteenth century American Windsors. From contemporary references in newspaper advertising and in orders from clients, it is obvious that this type was a handy, taken-for-granted chair that could be put to work anywhere, in or out of doors. They date after 1780.

Produced in sets, they were made in quantity and with some variations. With some the U-shaped bow has straight sides; others, like the chair illustrated, have a slight cyma curve, earning them the name "balloon back." Curved or straight, the back usually contains seven to nine shaped spindles, often with tiers of bamboo ringing. The seat is a modified shield shape and somewhat saddled. Flaring legs are turned with double bobbins that are ringed.

80

Illustration 23   *—Ginsburg & Levy, Inc.*

LOOP-BACK WINDSORS WITH BRACED BACKS

These two chairs are fine examples of the sophisticated version of the loop-back design. Matching chairs, they have seven spindle backs with all spindles, including the bracing ones, made tapering and enhanced by an element of vase shaping near the lower ends. They have shield-shaped saddled seats and the flaring legs have the bold vase turning and concave tapering foot typical of Windsors made in Rhode Island. They date from the late eighteenth century.

82

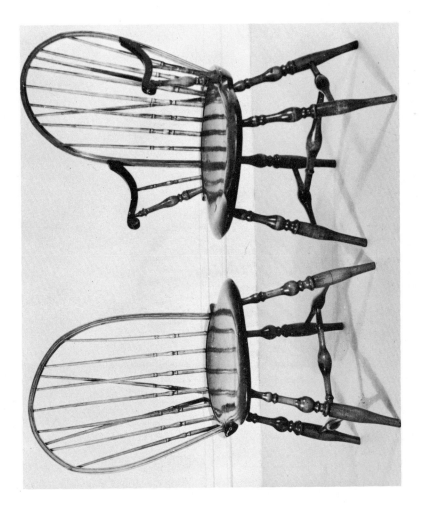

Illustration 24   *—The H. F. Du Pont Winterthur Museum*

LOOP-BACK CHAIR WITH UPHOLSTERED SEAT

Some of the Windsor chairmakers of Philadelphia, New York and, occasionally, Connecticut produced chairs, like the one illustrated, with seat upholstered in either fabric or leather. This was mostly done with side and armchairs of the loop-back type, but there is a record of an arch-back set made by John DeWitt of New York with upholstered seats. One of the chairs bears DeWitt's label and that of William W. Galatian, upholsterer, who did the covering with leather. When upholstery was used, it was done over a solid wooden seat with material held in place by tacks along the lower edge.

84

Illustration 25 —Israel Sack, Inc.

ROD-BACK WINDSOR ARMCHAIR

Chairs of the rod-back type made their appearance about 1800 and continued to be made for some thirty years. They marked a distinct break in design and structure with the Windsor tradition of the eighteenth century since they had neither continuous arm nor bow. They were often made in sets of one or two armchairs and from five to ten side chairs for use in dining rooms, living rooms and business offices, such as the director's room at Stephen Girard's bank in Philadelphia.

The back was formed of spindles surmounted by a flat shaped crest rail or one turned like the spindles. The outer spindles of the back were partially flattened. The cyma curved arms that might be of mahogany, were left natural and terminated in rolled ends. Legs were lighter with less splay, had bamboo turnings and were braced by a box stretcher.

86

Illustration 26   *—Dr. George P. Coopernail*

ROD-BACK ARMCHAIR WITH COMB-PIECE

Like the previous chair, this has the same seven-spindle back and flat crest rail. Above it is a rectangular comb piece supported by five spindles that pass through the crest rail. The shaped cyma curved arms are tenon-joined to the outer back spindles and end with a pronounced downward roll. The saddled seat is rectangular and somewhat shield shaped. The legs have only a medium flare, are plainly turned and have a box stretcher.

The rockers are probably a later addition although a few rod-back armchairs were made originally as rockers. The provenance of this chair is difficult to determine but it is probably of New England origin, made by a Windsor craftsman working in a small town.

88

Illustration 27   —*Israel Sack, Inc.*

ROD-BACK SIDE CHAIR WITH SEVEN
SPINDLE BACK

Judging by the number that have survived, rod-back side chairs of this type were made in large quantities in all sections of the country. Many matching sets of four or more are still available and are more desirable of course than just one odd chair. The slightly flaring sloping back is formed of two slightly larger outer spindles, connected by a turned crest rail, which flank seven slender tapering plain spindles with ring turnings. The slightly saddled seat is nearly rectangular. Legs, with only slight flare, are of plain turning with ringing. They are braced by a box stretcher of plain parts.

This side chair probably dates about 1825. Windsors of such simple lines were made by both city and country craftsmen. Its lines and structure show the influence of the Sheraton fancy chair.

90

Illustration 28   —*John K. Byard*

ROD-BACK CHAIR WITH STEP-DOWN
CREST RAIL

This chair differs from the preceding one in the shaping of its flat crest rail and the more pronounced slope of the back which has a slightly greater flare. The crest rail is supported by turned members that are flattened on the front. The seven tapering spindles are ring turned as are the plainly turned legs and stretcher parts. The seat is slightly saddled and almost rectangular. The chair, which is 37 inches tall, is painted black and retains the original stencil decoration of the crest rail. It is of New England provenance and dates before 1825.

Illustration 29   *—James B. O'Conner*

ARROW-BACK ARMCHAIR

The arrow-back Windsor which came about ten years after the rod-back marks an even further break with the eighteenth century types in that the back spindles were replaced by from three to five arrow-shaped vertical back splats, a further influence of the Sheraton fancy chair then being made in large quantities. So much so that some Windsor chairmakers also advertised as fancy chair makers. The general lines of the arrow-back were approximately the same as the rod-back chairs.

The back of the chair illustrated has a comfortable reverse curve. It is formed of a flat crest rail supported by two turned stiles which flank four arrow-shaped, flattened back splats that give the chair its name. The cyma curved arms terminate in rolled ends. The seat approximates the rectangular and has rounded front corners. This chair dates between 1810 and 1835. It was made in all sections in the shops of Windsor chairmakers who produced it by early mass-production methods.

94

ARROW-BACK ROCKER WITH COMB-PIECE

We know that a considerable proportion of the arrow-back Windsors were provided originally with rockers like this chair. It is unusual in that its back is surmounted by a rectangular comb-piece supported by five tapering spindles socketed into the upper edge of the crest rail. The back is formed by four flattened arrow-shaped splats that are turned at lower ends. The shaped arms are cyma-curved and terminate in rolled ends. The slightly saddled seat is rectangular with bowed front. The legs which have only a slight flare are of plain turnings with some bamboo ringing and are braced by a box stretcher of plain turned members. These are placed high enough above the rockers to indicate that the latter are original with the chair and not a later addition.

Of New England origin, this rocker dates approximately 1820–1830. It is painted black and retains its original gilt and stencil decoration.

Illustration 31   *—Author's Collection*

ARROW-BACK SIDE CHAIR WITH ROCKERS

Arrow-back side chairs, like the one illustrated, were made by the early chair shops from about 1810 to 1835 in all sections in sets or sometimes as rockers. This chair, with seat only 15 inches from the floor, is of the reduced size, made for a small person. Its shaped crest rail is supported by outer spindles with reverse curve and flattened on the front. The back is fitted with four flat arrow-shaped splats with turned lower ends. The seat is rectangular with curved front and is slightly saddled. The legs, plainly turned with bamboo ringing, are braced by a box stretcher of plain members. It is a light, easily handled chair. Judging by the numbers that have survived, fewer of these arrow-back side chairs were produced than similar ones of the rod-back type.

Illustration 32   —*Harry Shaw Newman*

THE FIREHOUSE WINDSOR

The name "Firehouse Windsor" was given a chair of this type close to fifty years ago since they were characteristic of furnishings of the houses of the old volunteer fire companies. They were also widely used in business places, lodge rooms and hotels. In its form the chair is a debased revival of the eighteenth century low-back. Its heavy U-shaped arm with crested back is supported by seven spindles, all of the same size, decorated with some ring turning. The slightly saddled seat is U-shaped. The plainly turned legs have little flare and are braced by a box stretcher, the front member of which can be a horizontal splat. Seat and continuous arm are of pine; turned parts are maple or yellow birch.

Chairs of this type were always factory made and were produced all along the Atlantic seaboard, especially in New England, New York and possibly as far west as Chicago, from about 1850 to 1870. The original finish was grained painting augmented by striping done in a darker color.

100

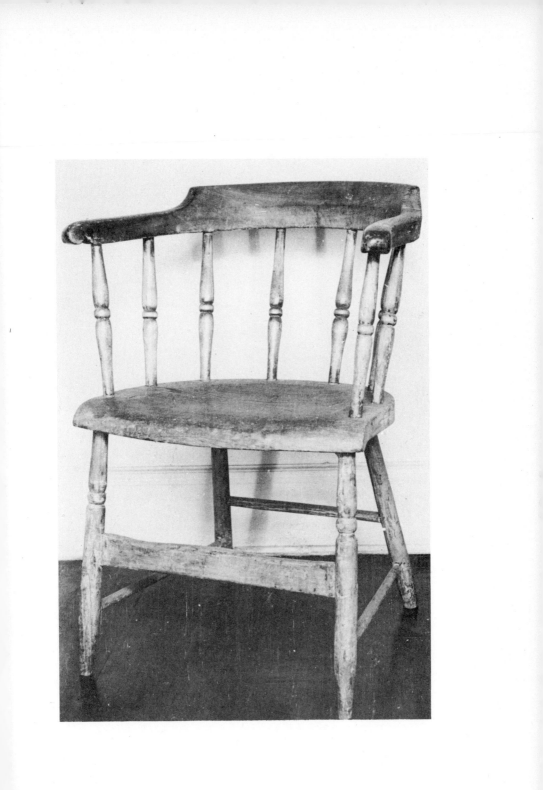

Illustration 33   *—Henry Clay Antiques*

CAPTAIN'S CHAIR

The name derives from its use in the pilot houses of boats that plied the Mississippi and coastal waters. Here sat the captain as he supervised the piloting of his craft. Captain's chairs date about twenty-five years later than those of the firehouse type from which they were patterned.

The chief difference is that the continuous arm is curved downward and socketed into the seat. The latter is thinner and has little or no saddling. Sometimes it is made of two or three pieces glued together. The legs have some ring turning but scarcely any flare. They are braced by a box stretcher, the front member of which is often ring-turned. Some later examples have woven cane instead of solid wood seats. Captain's chairs were factory made in large quantities as late as 1900. In addition to use in pilot houses, they were favorites in a variety of places where need was for a sturdy inexpensive chair, such as country hotels, court houses, school rooms and business offices.

Today they rate only as useful semi-antiques. They are once more being made in considerable quantity and are advertised in home furnishing magazines.

102

Illustration 34

SURVIVAL LOOP-BACK SIDE CHAIR

Such chairs were factory made in large quantities from before 1880 to about 1900. They are interesting as survivals of the loop-back type though not collectible as antiques. They were widely used from Sunday school rooms to meeting places as well as in boarding house dining rooms and many kitchens—practically any place where the need was for a strong chair that would stand hard use. In their day they sold for about a dollar. They were made of cheap grades of oak, ash or maple or an assortment of hard woods. The somewhat U-shaped seat was not saddled and was often made of several pieces. The original finish was varnish.

Illustration 35

FACTORY MADE BOW-BACK WINDSOR

About 1900 some American furniture factories revived the production of bow-back Windsor armchairs. The chair illustrated is a typical example. Although the intention was to make chairs like those done by old methods, because of factory production they were not complete copies.

The differences are a thicker continuous arm and heavier spindles; the seat, often of two or three pieces, is not as thick and has little or no saddling. Only the front legs are baluster turned. Similarly turning of the stretcher members is plainer. Since some chairs of this sort have been used long enough to acquire some age, they are sometimes mistaken for original ones. Hence this chair is illustrated *not* as a collectible antique but as a warning to the unwary. These factory-made bow-back chairs were favored for public library reading rooms, Y.M.C.A. lounges and kindred places including hotel porches and lobbies.

Illustration 36   *—Author's Collection*

THE BOSTON ROCKER

Although at first glance the Boston rocker seems to be a separate chair form from the Windsor, it is a cousin of the rod-back. As such it is included as an example of how the Sheraton fancy chair affected Windsor chairmaking in America. The resemblance between it and the rod-back can be seen in the shaped crest rail, the back formed of seven tapering spindles and the cyma-curved arms, all of which are done in the best tradition of the rod-back armchair, though with slight variations.

This Windsor relationship is further amplified in the Salem rocker which has an oval solid pine seat as compared with that of the Boston rocker with its pine seat upcurved at the rear and boldly rolled at front. Like rod-back chairs, it has a painted finish augmented with stencil gilding done in the fancy chair manner. Boston and Salem rockers were made from about 1820 to 1850 in New England chair shops. Some of these shifted from rod-back Windsors to specializing in Boston rockers.

Illustration 37   —Israel Sack, Inc.

LOW-BACK WINDSOR WRITING CHAIR

The Windsor writing chair with its broad writing tablet originated in America. It made its appearance in the Pre-Revolutionary period, probably about 1760 and continued to be made in the various types for nearly a century. Because of their special structure, production of them was much more limited than the standard types. Presumably each writing chair was made as a special order. Consequently they are among the Windsor rarities today.

This low-back writing chair is typical of Philadelphia workmanship. The elliptical writing tablet is supported by three vase turned spindles that are socketed into a side extension of the seat. Made before 1775, it shows how neatly the standard low-back design could be augmented.

110

COMB-BACK WINDSOR WRITING CHAIR

Of Pennsylvania provenance and dating about 1760, it has a tall back formed by six spindles surmounted by a serpentine shaped comb-piece. The broad elliptical writing tablet which forms part of the continuous arm has a small drawer beneath, presumably for quill pens. There is a second and larger drawer beneath the seat for other writing materials. The seat has an extension that serves as anchorage for the three baluster turned spindles that support the writing arm.

112

Illustration 39   *—Israel Sack, Inc.*

BOW-BACK WINDSOR WRITING CHAIR

Bow-back writing chairs, as with the chair illustrated, sometimes have a back surmounted by a comb-piece; others were made without it. Here the loop-shaped writing tablet is anchored to the upper surface of the continuous arm with one end of the bow passing through it. There are two small drawers, one beneath the arm and the other under the seat. The baluster turned spindles that support the writing tablet are socketed into side extensions of the seat. Concave taper of lower ends of the legs indicate that this chair is of Rhode Island provenance, dating before 1775.

114

Illustration 40   —Ginsburg & Levy, Inc.

ARCH-BACK WINDSOR WRITING CHAIR

A rare and most unusual writing chair. There is a question as to whether it was made originally with a writing arm or whether the tablet was attached to a chair of standard design and braced by two additional spindles canted forward from the seat at a wide angle. With its rockers that could be original or attached later, its design is remarkable. Note that the seat is without an extension for spindles supporting the writing area. It is a New England chair of the late eighteenth century.

116

Illustration 41   *—I. M. Wiese*

ROD-BACK WINDSOR WRITING CHAIR

This chair follows the lines of a rod-back armchair in general structure except that the writing tablet is so shaped that it replaces the right arm. It has a nine spindle back and a flat slightly concave crest rail. The arm has both a small drawer beneath and an attached candle bracket that is pivoted. The U-shaped seat with straight front has a side extension that supports the three canted spindles supporting the tablet. The crest rail of the back still retains some traces of the original painted decoration. It is a New England chair of the early nineteenth century.

118

LEFT-HANDED WRITING WINDSOR

This chair of the rod-back type is, as far as can be determined, the only left-handed writing chair in any American collection. It dates about 1825 and is of maple, pine and hickory, painted red. The large writing tablet replaces the left arm and is supported by four sloping spindles anchored in the seat which has an ample extension. Otherwise the chair has the details characteristic of rod-back armchairs with a seven-spindle back, shaped crest rail and right arm terminating in a rolled end. Legs are bamboo turned and taper at both ends. The front member of the box stretcher has a rectangular flat section. Other stretcher members have plain turnings.

Illustration 43

ARROW-BACK WRITING WINDSOR

Writing Windsors of the arrow-back type are unusual. As very few have survived, it may be presumed that not many were made. This chair is unusually tall. The back has a double shaped crest rail and six arrow-shaped back splats. The writing tablet with boldly curved outline replaces the right arm and is supported by three plain spindles socketed into the seat extension. The other arm terminates in a boldly curved rolled end. The simple turned legs have little flare and are equipped with a box stretcher, the front member of which is vase-and-ball turned. This chair dates about 1825.

Illustration 44   *—Warren W. Creamer*

FIREHOUSE WRITING WINDSOR

When Windsor chairs became factory work, making them as writing chairs was limited indeed. The chair illustrated is the only example of which there is any record. It follows the lines of other chairs of its kind with the addition of the elliptical writing tablet which has an inset pewter inkwell. There is a small drawer beneath and a second one under the seat.

The chair which retains some of its original paint, was made about 1850. Originally it belonged to Franklin K. Pierce, Fourteenth President of the United States who gave it to William Butterfield, editor and publisher of the Concord, New Hampshire *Daily Patriot*.

124

Illustration 45   *—Ginsburg & Levy, Inc.*

COMB-BACK WINDSOR HIGH CHAIR

Windsor chairmakers started early to make children's high chairs, producing them as comb-back chairs like the one illustrated. They were made consistently with seat about 21 inches from the floor. The longer legs were given additional flare for stability needed when a small occupant, as might be expected, started squirming. This chair has a seven-spindle back surmounted by a comb-piece with carved ears. It has blunt-arrow legs with long vase-turned upper elements. An unusual feature is the restraining rod that passes through the upper ends of the baluster-turned supports of the continuous arm. A typical Pennsylvania chair, dating before 1775, it is 40 inches tall.

Illustration 46   *—Israel Sack, Inc.*

BOW-BACK WINDSOR HIGH CHAIR

This high chair with seven-spindle back has all the details of a standard size but was made in miniature. The much longer legs have fine baluster turning which matches the supports of the continuous arm. The chair is of New England provenance and dates about 1770.

128

Illustration 47   *—Charlotte & Edgar Sittig*

LOOP-BACK WINDSOR HIGH CHAIR

This rural Pennsylvania high chair with five-spindle back is characteristic of the loop-back type. Made in the late eighteenth century, it has a plain U-shaped bow and the shaped arms are cyma curved, terminating in a bold downward roll. The modified shield shaped seat has little saddling. The tall legs are of double bobbin turning with bamboo ringing. Attached to the front legs is a well worn footrest placed about eight inches below the seat.

Illustration 48   —*The H. F. Du Pont Winterthur Museum*

ARCH-BACK WINDSOR HIGH CHAIR

This high chair with seven-spindle back is an unusually fine example of its type. Like a full size arch-back, it has a nicely bent bow that terminates in short flat arms. The seven spindles of the back are bobbin shaped about a third of the way from the seat. The boldly turned arm supports are done with the same detail as the tall legs. The seat is nicely shaped and well saddled. A New England chair, probably of Massachusetts origin, it dates between 1765 and 1780.

132

Illustration 49   *—L. T. Hunt*

ROD-BACK WINDSOR HIGH CHAIR

From the numbers that have survived, high chairs of the rod-back type were made in considerably greater volume than earlier ones. The chair illustrated is typical of the rod-back in high chair form. It has a five-spindle back and short turned arms. The seat is rectangular and the long legs have bamboo ringing. Chairs like this were made in all sections and date after 1800.

134

Illustration 50   *—Israel Sack, Inc.*

FIREHOUSE WINDSOR HIGH CHAIR

Here we have the early factory-produced Windsor in high chair form. It dates after 1850. Like the large chairs of this type, it has a U-shaped continuous arm that surmounts eight spindles all alike that are ring turned at the center. The U-shaped seat is plain. The tall legs are ring-turned in front and terminate in small button feet. Those at the rear are plain. There is a footrest attached at front. The legs have some flare and are braced by a box stretcher.

136

Illustration 51   —*Lillian Blankley Cogan*

COMB-BACK WINDSOR CHILD'S CHAIR

Besides high chairs the Windsor chairmakers also made reduced-size chairs for older children. These can be distinguished from high chairs with sawed off legs by completeness of leg turnings and proper placing of bracing stretcher. The chair illustrated is a typical comb-back of about 1750–1760 with untouched blunt-arrow legs terminating in ball feet. From its size, it was made for a child between five and ten years old. It has a seven-spindle back surmounted by a well shaped comb-piece. The U-shaped seat is well saddled and the H-shaped stretcher has bulbously turned side members.

Illustration 52   *—Lillian Blankley Cogan*

BOW-BACK WINDSOR CHILD'S CHAIR

This chair with its tall bow and seven-spindle back has the same lines and details of construction as a full size chair of this type. The well-done turning of the arm supports and legs indicate that it is a New England chair made before 1775. Its elliptical seat is somewhat saddled. This chair is branded "H. Cate." When and where he worked has not as yet been established.

Illustration 53   —*The H. F. Du Pont Winterthur Museum*

ARCH-BACK CHILD'S CHAIR

With its five-spindle back this chair also has a pair of bracing spindles as with chairs of full size. It has the characteristic nicely bent hoop that terminates in short flat arms. The seat is shield shaped with projecting rear tailpiece for the bracing spindles. The flaring legs are of double bobbin turning. Members of the H-shaped stretcher have bamboo ringing. It is a late eighteenth century New England chair.

CHILD'S FIREHOUSE WINDSOR CHAIR

Making small Windsors for children persisted even after the advent of factory workmanship as shown by this very small chair of the firehouse type. Its design and construction are identical with those made in full size. This chair was factory-made between 1850 and 1860. One of a pair, it is small enough to have been made either as a doll's chair or a salesman sample. It has its original light brown paint trimmed with broad stripes of darker brown.

Illustration 55   *—Museum of Fine Arts, Boston*

LOW-BACK WINDSOR SETTEE

Settees were made by the Windsor chairmakers from as early as the low-back and comb-back years through those of the rod-back type. As far as is known they did not make either arrow-back or firehouse settees. Settees were used on piazzas, in gardens and indoors in halls and living rooms as well as for public buildings. Some were in the love-seat size; others were long enough to have six, eight or even ten legs.

This low-back settee of Philadelphia provenance dates before 1775. Here the continuous arm terminates in boldly carved knuckle ends and is surmouneted by a cresting the full length of the back. This is formed by 38 short spindles each with centeral bulge. The outer spindles, of larger diameter, are vase-turned and set with a forward rake. The rectangular seat is slightly saddled and supported by eight vase-turned legs that are braced by a multiple recessed stretcher with boldly done ball-and-ring turnings.

146

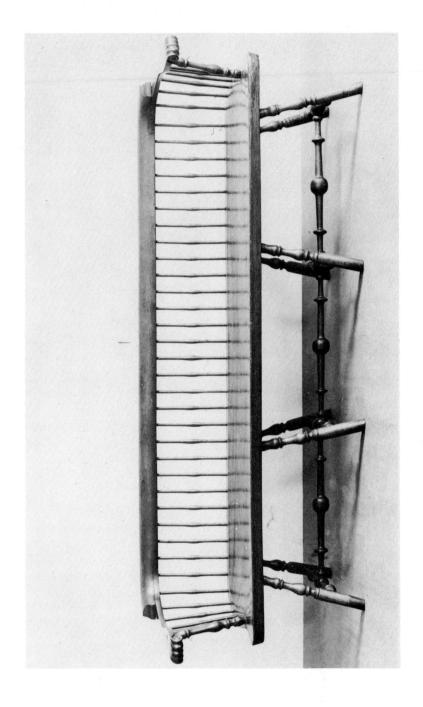

COMB-BACK WINDSOR SETTEE

This settee is over seven feet long and has a well-shaped comb-piece with volute carved ears supported by 31 tall spindles. These are flanked by six shorter ones. All spindles have bobbin shaping below the continuous arm which has vase turned outer spindles and terminates in bold knuckle carved hand grips. The broad seat is slightly saddled and is supported by ten vase-turned legs of the Massachusetts type. These are braced by a multiple recessed stretcher with ring and bulbous turning.

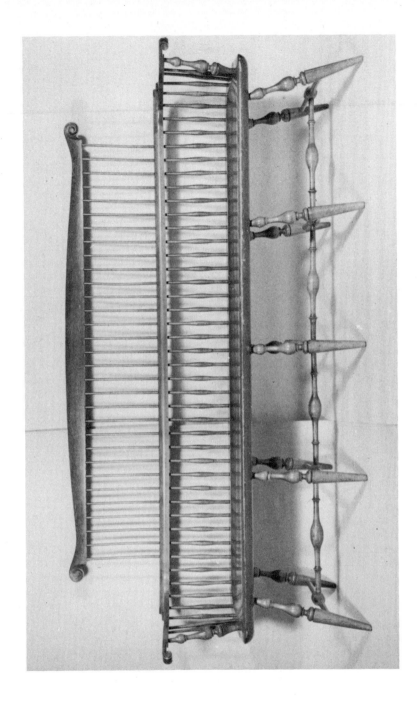

Illustration 57   —*The H. F. Du Pont Winterthur Museum*

BOW-BACK WINDSOR SETTEE

With its triple bow-back this settee is the· rarest of its type. It shows what niceties of construction could be accomplished in such a piece. The central bow is slightly higher than those flanking it with the ends interlaced. The back contains 23 tall tapering spindles that pass through the continuous arm and are flanked by six shorter ones. The arm is crested and terminates in knuckle carving. The ends are supported by vase-turned spindles with forward rake. The seat has some saddling and is supported by ten flaring legs which are vase-turned and braced by a multiple recessed stretcher turned with ring and bulbous elements. It is an eighteenth century New England piece of unusual charm.

150

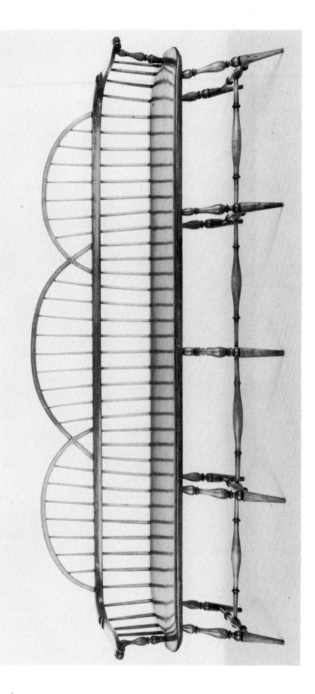

Illustration 58   *—John K. Byard*

LOOP-BACK WINDSOR SETTEE

This loop-back settee with back formed of 28 slightly tapering spindles contained within a nicely bent bow is 66 inches long. The shaped arms have a slight cyma curve and terminate with boldly rolled ends. The seat is slightly saddled and the eight legs have double bobbin shaping with bamboo ringing. They are braced by a multiple recessed stretcher with members slightly bulbous and bamboo ringed. It is a New England settee made about 1790–1800.

152

Illustration 59   *—Winifred E. Harding*

ROD-BACK WINDSOR SETTEE

Here we have the rod-back chair expanded into a settee but staying as close as its size allows to the design of an armchair of the rod-back type. Its 27-spindle back has a flat shaped crest rail which is supported at its outer ends by turned uprights. It has simple arms made of turned parts. The long seat has slight saddling and is supported by eight simple turned legs braced by a plain box stretcher. Spindles, arms, legs and other turned parts are made slightly decorative by use of repeated bamboo ringing. This settee dates ca. 1800–1820.

154

Illustration 60   *—Ginsburg & Levy, Inc.*

WINDSOR CRADLE

Cradles are the rarest examples of Windsor craftsmanship. From the few that have survived we know that they were all made with rockers and while some had hoods, others did not. The cradle illustrated has an elaborate hood made of spindle-turned members. Head and foot are formed with boldly bent hoops like those of a loop-back chair and are fitted with bamboo turned spindles that are repeated for the sides. Except for rockers and bottom, this cradle was made entirely of turned spindles and bent members. It is of late eighteenth century Boston provenance and bears the label of Saver & Frost. This reads in part: "WARRANTED/WINDSOR CHAIRS/and SET-TEES/in the newest stile and of superior quality/Made and sold by/SEAVER & FROST/Sign of the WINDSOR CHAIR/No. 57 . . . . . Street, BOSTON."

156

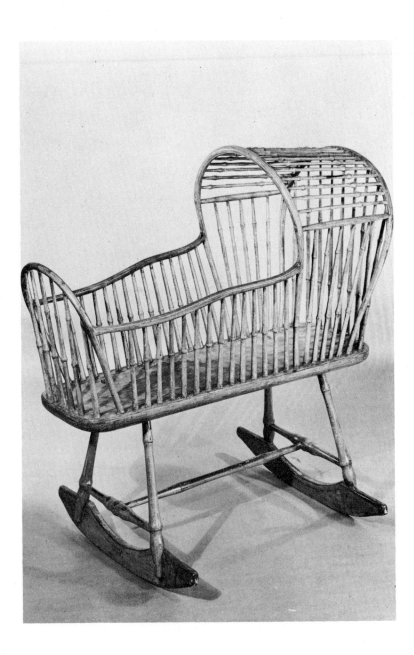

Illustration 61   *—Philadelphia Museum of Art*

THREE-LEG WINDSOR TABLE

Not many tables made by the Windsor craftsmen have survived. They are of two kinds, three legged and four legged. This table with circular dish top and three vase-turned legs is presumably of Philadelphia origin of the late eighteenth century. It is recorded that it once belonged to the artist Thomas Sully who used it beside his easel for paints and brushes.

Illustration 62

FOUR-LEG WINDSOR TABLE

Such tables were made with either oval or rectangular tops. The table illustrated has an oval one. Its vase-turned legs are braced top and bottom by box stretchers with plain members. The legs are not socketed into the top but tenon-joined to flat cross members to which the top is attached. It is a late eighteenth century piece presumably of New England provenance.

160

Illustration 63

A WINDSOR STOOL

With minor variations, such stools were made by Windsor craftsmen from the late eighteenth century until about 1830. There are
two types, three-leg and four-leg. Usually the legs have vase-shaped
turning and some are stretcher-braced. Tops are most frequently
circular though a few are oval or rectangular with rounded corners.
From the concave taper of its legs, the stool illustrated appears to be
of Rhode Island origin.

SHOP OF DAVID ALLING, MAKER OF WINDSOR
AND FANCY CHAIRS

Painted ca. 1840 by an unknown artist, it depicts the Alling shop and house that stood on Broad Street, Newark, N.J. Alling is shown in his shirt sleeves standing in the doorway of his workshop. Although painted toward the close of the Windsor period this is the only painting known of a Windsor chairmaker's shop.

Section IV

SOME HISTORIC AMERICAN WINDSORS

Although documented facts are fragmentary, it is evident that Windsor chairs played a part in some important events of American history. These largely center about the sessions of the Continental Congress and the Signing of the Declaration of Independence. The locale was the Assembly Chamber in the Pennsylvania Provincial State House, better known as Independence Hall.

The first session in 1775 of the Continental Congress was so hurriedly convened that it had to meet in Carpenter's Hall. The members probably sat in Windsor chairs for, although proof is lacking, it is generally considered that this meeting place was furnished with them, presumably made by Richmond, first name unknown, but one of the first Philadelphia craftsmen to specialize in making Windsors only.

The next year the Continental Congress moved to the Assembly Chamber on the ground floor of Independence Hall. Here some, if not all, the delegates sat in Windsors for there is a record that Francis Trumble, a leading Philadelphia Windsor chairmaker, was paid £6/14/0 on May 31, 1776 for twelve chairs and two tables. These chairs obviously were in use on July 4th when the members of the Congress arose to affix their signatures to that highly revolutionary document. What became of the chairs used that day is unknown since during the British occupation of Philadelphia, 1777-1778, they used Independence Hall as a combination hospital and prison. None of the furnishings there are known to have survived. Some may have been chopped up for firewood by the prison guards.

When the British evacuated Philadelphia and the Continental Congress returned and once more sat in Independence Hall, it had been refurnished. This refurbishing is known to have included a good number of Windsor chairs. To wit, Francis Trumble in August and November of that year received two payments, £64/8/6 and £84/15/0 for "round back armchairs, ditto plain, ditto low back and sack back." At the low prices then current for Windsors, under one pound each, these must have been payments for close to 150 Windsor chairs. These with some additions and replacements were furnishings of the Assembly chamber at Independence Hall throughout the remaining sessions of the Continental Congress and of the Constitutional Convention which lasted from May 25 to September 17, 1787, during which time the Constitution of the United States was drafted.

One of these Windsors, branded F T, has survived and has been returned to Independence Hall (see Illustration 66). The history of the chair is as follows: In 1802 when the capital of Pennsylvania was moved to Harrisburg, the furnishings of Independence Hall were shipped there for use by the legislature. This continued until about 1814 when this furniture, probably the worse for long usage and some moving around, was sold at auction. At that time one of the chairs was bought by a member of the Esterhazy family, who retained ownership of it for several generations.

In addition to these Windsors supplied by Francis Trumble, records show that other Philadelphia craftsmen supplied Windsor chairs, settees and benches for Independence Hall. These include the benches, probably for spectators at the rear of the chamber, that were bought from Michael Kuntz in 1778; two settees supplied by John Pinkerton in 1779 and chairs made by Joseph Henzey in 1791.

170

The nearest we have to a pictorial representation of the actual Signing on July 4, 1776 is the painting "Congress Voting Independence" by Robert Edge Pine (see Illustration 66). Pine was an Englishman who migrated to the United States in 1784, having already an established reputation for portraits and historical paintings. He came here with the avowed purpose of doing several paintings of the leading events of the American Revolution. He began with this one. When he died suddenly of apoplexy in 1788, it was unfinished but was completed shortly thereafter by Edward Savage. To paint this historical scene, Pine obtained the use of the Assembly chamber in which the Signing took place and depicted this interior with its original architectural trim, which was altered somewhat later.

Pine knew most of the Signers personally and his painting caused much favorable comment. Apparently it was approved by the Signers themselves, most of whom were still alive. From the point of Windsor history, this painting shows at least one chair as it was used in Independence Hall. It depicts Benjamin Franklin in the center foreground seated sidewise in a bow-back armchair of the sort known to have been made for this room by Francis Trumble. It could well have been painted from one of his "sack back" chairs. In fact it is the same type as the one now in Independence Hall that is branded F T.

Even before its signing, the Declaration of Independence and a Windsor chair were closely associated, for Thomas Jefferson wrote the first draft of it seated in his comb-back writing chair (see Frontispiece). This chair and Jefferson's first draft of the Declaration are both in the collection of the American Philosophical Society in Philadelphia. Jefferson was president of the Society for eighteen years.

His writing Windsor has been slighted, not to say snubbed by some writers because in their opinion it possesses "de-

171

merits in style" since the seat seems to have been rebuilt so that it revolves and the writing tablet apparently is an addition. Jefferson was an able architect as shown by his beloved Monticello and the Virginia State Capitol at Richmond. He also loved to design things for his creature comforts and showed considerable ingenuity in so doing. There is every indication that he designed his writing Windsor, had it made according to his own ideas and disregarded the current fashion. This is obvious when it is compared with a standard Philadelphia comb-back of the period, all of which had U-shaped seats and were not made to revolve.

The only other record of Windsors for public use (see Illustration 38) in the Revolutionary or Post Revolutionary periods occurred in New York City. Here John DeWitt was paid £29/14/0, November 14, 1796 for Windsors that he had been commissioned to make for use in Federal Hall when that building was altered and refurnished for the Federal government at the time New York was temporarily the capital of the United States. It was on the portico of Federal Hall that Washington took his oath of office as our first President.

That George Washington owned Windsor chairs is well documented. It concerned some he bought in Philadelphia and had shipped to Mount Vernon when he was nearing the end of his second presidential term. On May 14, 1796, he bought twenty-four "oval back" chairs from Gilbert and Robert Gaw, Philadelphia Windsor chairmakers for which he paid them $44.00. On May 17 they sold him three more for $4.00, making a total purchase of twenty-seven chairs for $48.00. Thus, these chairs cost Washington a fraction of a cent over $1.61 each, showing how inexpensive loop-back Windsors were in 1796. It is known that at the time of his death in 1799, there were thirty Windsors on the portico at Mount Vernon.

There is a simple loop-back side chair with a seven-spindle

172

back and bamboo turnings in the Mount Vernon collection now that is presumed to have belonged to Washington. Although it bears no maker's brand, it is believed to have been one of the chairs purchased from Gilbert and Robert Gaw (see Illustration 67). The Mount Vernon collection also includes another slightly varying loop-back side chair with a Washington history. It belonged to him while living in Philadelphia during his second presidential term, at the close of which some of his household furnishings were sold at auction. Besides this chair Mount Vernon has a bow-back Windsor high chair (see Illustration 68). Presumably it was used by Martha Washington's grandchildren, Nellie and George Washington Parke Custis who lived there as part of the family group after their adoption by George Washington.

Finally, there is at Mount Vernon a two-wheel riding chair with a Windsor chair seat but in place of flaring turned legs it is supported by plain iron ones bolted to the carriage frame. This unique conveyance has a complete history tracing it back to Thomas, Sixth Lord Fairfax who was Washington's patron in his youth and early manhood. Lord Fairfax came to this country in 1735 and by 1750 had established himself at Greenway Court where he died in 1781, thus dating this riding chair some years prior to the latter date. It is included in the Mount Vernon collection because it is known that Washington owned such a conveyance and in 1774 bought another for his mother at a cost of £40. Forerunner of the nineteenth century buggy, the two-wheeled riding chair drawn by one horse was the vehicle of everyday use in eighteenth century Virginia. It was more serviceable than four-wheeled carriages since many of the roads were little more than cleared spaces running through the woodlands. Lord Fairfax's is the only riding chair that has survived. It proves another use of the Windsor and a very early one for a chair of the rod-back type.

173

Washington was not the only prominent American who was partial to Windsors when the need was for chairs "strong enough for common sitting." The second President of the United States, John Adams, had his favorite Windsor (see Illustration 70). For over fifty years it has been in the collection of the Quincy Historical Society and on display in the John Quincy Adams birthplace, Quincy, Mass. It has long been labeled "John Adams' Favorite Chair" and was presented to the Society by a member of the Adams family. It is a bow-back armchair with unusually tall back. Closeness to the floor of its recessed H-stretcher would seem to indicate that sometime in the past the legs were shortened. This is understandable when it is remembered that John Adams and his son John Quincy were less than average height and that either father or son had two inches or more cut off the legs to make it comfortable enough to become a favorite chair.

Another historic Windsor is a fan-back armchair with braced five-spindle back on long term loan to the Museum of Fine Arts, Boston (see Illustration 71). This chair belonged to Tutor Henry Flint, much beloved by Harvard students and graduates alike during his long period on its faculty, 1699-1760. By his will his "easy green chair" was bequeathed to his niece Dorothy who had provided a study and bedroom for her uncle in the Quincy mansion. The chair later passed by inheritance to Dr. Oliver Wendell Holmes and thence to his son and namesake Mr. Justice Holmes of the United States Supreme Court.

As far as is known Royal White Hart Masonic Lodge No. 2, Halifax, North Carolina, is the only one with a set of Windsor chairs still in use which was made for it in the eighteenth century. These comprise a set of eight fan-back chairs with seven-spindle backs (see Illustration 72). According to the minutes of 1770, a committee was empowered to buy "eight chairs for the Masonic Brotherhood from Richard

Hall." The entire set has been carefully preserved and still bears traces of the original paint, black with gilt striping. These chairs are in the lodge room of its building on Saint David Street, the first in America built and used continuously for Masonic purposes.

Illustration 65   —*Independence National Historical Park Collection*

INDEPENDENCE HALL BOW-BACK WINDSOR OF 1778

Made by Francis Trumble and branded F T this is the only chair used by members of the Continental Congress and the Constitutional Convention that has survived. Chairs of the same type also made by Trumble were in use when the Declaration of Independence was signed.

176

Illustration 66   *—The Pennsylvania Historical Society*

"CONGRESS VOTING INDEPENDENCE"

This historical scene was painted by Robert Edge Pine about 1785 in the Assembly chamber where the Declaration was signed. In the center foreground Benjamin Franklin is sitting sidewise in a bow-back Windsor of the kind made by Francis Trumble, Philadelphia chairmaker.

A WASHINGTON "OVAL" WINDSOR CHAIR

In May 1796 he bought 27 of these loop-back chairs from Gilbert and Robert Gaw, Philadelphia Windsor chairmakers for use at Mount Vernon after he retired from the presidency of the United States.

Illustration 68   *—The Mount Vernon Ladies' Association*

BOW-BACK WINDSOR HIGH CHAIR AT
MOUNT VERNON

As Mrs. Washington's grandchildren, Nellie and George Washington Parke Custis, were part of the Washington family such a chair was provided for them in their babyhood.

179

Illustration 69   *—The Mount Vernon Ladies' Association*

LORD FAIRFAX'S RIDING CHAIR

The only vehicle of its kind that has survived, it dates sometime before 1781 and is like one owned by Washington. Here the seat is a rod-back Windsor side chair supported by strap-iron legs.

Illustration 70   *—Quincy Historical Society*

PRESIDENT JOHN ADAMS' FAVORITE CHAIR

This bow-back Windsor with tall back so labeled came from a member of the Adams family over 50 years ago. Notice that the legs have been cut off, probably intentionally since John Adams and his son were little over five feet tall.

181

Illustration 71   *—Museum of Fine Arts, Boston*

TUTOR HENRY FLYNT'S "EASY GREEN CHAIR"

He taught at Harvard from 1699 to 1760 and was beloved by both students and graduates. By his will drawn in 1758 he left this chair to his niece Mrs. Dorothy Jackson of Quincy, Mass. Later it was owned by Dr. Oliver Wendell Holmes and his son and namesake, for many years Associate Justice of the United States Supreme Court.

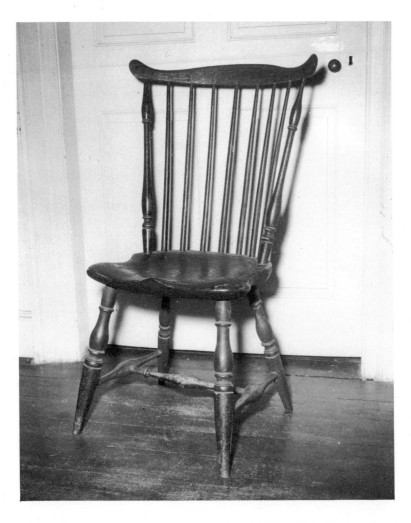

Illustration 72   *—Royal White Hart Lodge No. 2*

MASONIC FAN-BACK WINDSOR SIDE CHAIR

This is one of a set of eight chairs made in 1770 by Richard Hall for the Royal White Hart Lodge No. 2 of Halifax, N.C. The entire set are still used by the lodge that meets in the first building built in the United States exclusively for Masonic purposes.

183

Section V

ENGLISH WINDSOR CHAIRS

With all that has been written about English furniture for half a century or more, the Windsor chair has been given practically no consideration as a distinct form. The reasons are fairly obvious. First it was provincial in origin; second, practically nothing is known of its makers until after the start of the nineteenth century.

Yet, as already stated in Section I, its ancestor dates back to the fifteenth century at least, as shown by the Gothic three-leg chair still extant at Saint Cross Hospital near Winchester (see Illustration 73). From this crude type came simple but less heavy chairs made by sixteenth century wheelwrights in which the Windsor lines were apparent and developed further during the late seventeenth century.

By the start of the eighteenth century, a few surviving examples are witnesses to the fact that Windsors as we know them today were being made by provincial craftsmen, wheelwrights and those handy enough with wood-working tools to contrive chairs of Windsor structure for their own use. What they made then and for several decades was the plainest of "stick" chairs for farmhouse and tavern use (see Illustration 74). During this time and for the rest of the century research has established that the Windsor was a common chair form which was made at one or more places in Berkshire, Buckinghamshire, Lancashire, Norfolk, Somerset, Suffolk and Yorkshire, all essentially agricultural counties at the time. Some were also made in Wales and Scotland.

Some Windsors were made by craftsmen who fashioned

187

each part but far more were produced by workers who depended on chair parts—legs, spindles, stretchers, bows and seats—prepared in the rough by woodland workers who wrought as close as possible to where the trees were felled. When one timber stand had been reduced to chair parts, they moved on with their thatched work sheds to another timber spot. There is a record of such woodland workers, active about 1780 in Buckinghamshire, making chair parts that were shipped to London and towns as far away as Scotland.

These "bolgers," as the turner who worked with a pole lathe were called, made legs, bows, spindles and other turned parts while the "bottomers" shaped the planked seats. In the chair shops their work was augmented by "benchmen" who did the saddling of the seats and produced the back splats and other sawed parts. From them the work passed to the "framer" who assembled each chair from its finished parts. Next came the "polisher" who smoothed away all roughnesses with cutting tools and sandpaper. Then all chairs not left in the white, went to either the "stainer" who stained them an even color with his water-soluble dyes or the men who painted them either black or green.

These working ways of the English Windsor chairmakers were really a simple version of what it now called assembly line production and far different from the working ways then practiced in America. There a maker of Windsors aided by one or two journeymen and apprentices fashioned all parts of his chairs in his shop. He was his own turner, seat-maker and bender of curved parts.

English chairmakers knew from experience what available woods were most desirable for Windsors and used them consistently. Beech, ash and elm were favored woods. Beech which turned well and was available in quantity was used for legs, spindles and other turned parts. Seats were made of elm from two-inch planks sawed into blocks. For bow-comb-piece and other bent parts, ash was usual, but on finer chairs yew was used. Sawed parts, such as back splats, were often made of oak. Such were the woods generally used but antique English Windsors, usually of the finer quality, are known where walnut, cherry and other fruit woods were preferred. Also there were the very fine Windsors, presumably from the hands of London cabinetmakers where mahogany was used throughout. Such chairs, usually with four cabriole legs, cannot be considered as typical of England as a whole. Rather they were special chairs, made for the limited de luxe London market.

Extensive use of beech for Windsors connected their making with Buckinghamshire almost from the start. There the beech tree was so common that it was sometimes referred to as the "Buckinghamshire weed." Beech chair parts were produced there throughout most of the second half of the eighteenth century. But it was well into the first decade of the nineteenth century before the making of complete Windsors began in High Wycombe and one or two neighboring towns. From a modest start, High Wycombe, now in the process of being absorbed into the outer fringe of suburban London, soon was the leading center of Windsor chairmaking, a distinction it retained well into the present century with factory methods replacing hand craftsmanship.

By 1760, the types of Windsors made in England were pretty much standardized and remained so for about a century. They included five types, comb-back, bow-back, bow-back with comb, loop-back and rod-back. The low-back, so widely made in eighteenth century America, is missing from this list and examples, except of the Victorian period, do not seem to exist. Yet they were consistently made by eighteenth century American craftsmen. What is the explanation? The conjecture is that the low-back was a primitive country type which had already passed from favor and was copied in

189

America from stray imports that dated back to or before the start of the eighteenth century.

With English comb-back, bow-back and fan-back chairs, a striking characteristic of the back is the central splat, flanked on either side by from two to five plain spindles of the same length (see Illustration 75). The splat could be plain or pierced with scroll-shaped openings sometimes simple and at others elaborate (see Illustration 76). The latter with intricately pierced splats, including those where the back is formed by an arrangement of three splats, all pierced, are frequently referred to as Chippendale Windsors (see Illustration 77), not that they or any like them could have come from Thomas Chippendale's cabinetmaking shop but rather from the similarity of pattern piercing to be seen on claw-and-ball-foot chairs of the Chippendale period. Similarly, some are called "Gothick" because the piercing forms a pattern of gothic arch openings.

During the close of the eighteenth century and continuing into the nineteenth, the upper end of the back splat was pierced in a classic urn pattern or in a group of three feathers design known as Prince of Wales Feathers. The latter reflected the popularity of George, the Prince Regent. Both designs were characteristic of the contemporary Hepplewhite style. After 1820 came the wheel piercing pattern which retained its popularity to the end of the period in which English Windsors were produced by old handcraft methods.

Just as American Windsors have certain characteristics that clearly mark their provenance, there are easily recognized features that identify chairs bearing them as unquestionably English. Summarized, they are about as follows: The legs are socketed into the seat much closer to the edge and have considerably less rake than American examples. A chair with cabriole legs terminating in pad feet is an English Windsor (see Illustration 76 and 77). The one exception to this are the

190

very very few American Windsors with cabriole legs of eighteenth century Philadelphia provenance, most of which are now in museum collections. Seats of English Windsors are consistently shield-shaped or square, save for some of the Victorian period which are round and generally not as thick, having been cut from inch-and-a-half rather than two-inch planks.

Another English characteristic is the so-called "cowhorn and spur" stretcher (see Illustrations 78 and 79). Here it is curved in a deep concave arc from one front leg to the other and is joined to the rear legs by short turnings set at an angle. This stretcher construction was not used by American makers of Windsor chairs.

When after 1810, High Wycombe became the leading Windsor chair town of England, certain makers there established chair shops that continued for a considerable period. First of these were Thomas Widgington and Samuel Treacher, both experienced chairmakers of the vicinity. Actually the first Windsor chair shop in High Wycombe was started by Widgington in 1801 where he employed a few craftsmen and thus initiated Windsor chairmaking on a shop basis.

In time some of his workmen set up their own shops there and in neighboring villages. Prominent among these succeeding chairmakers were Daniel Glenister, Walter Skull and Benjamin North. Both the Glenister and Skull ventures were highly successful and continued until close to the end of the century. H. F. Goodchild whose shop was in neighboring Naphill was the last Windsor chair craftsman. His was never a large operation. He died in 1950 but long before that date Windsor chairmaking in High Wycombe had become factory work.

Illustration 73   *—St. Cross Hospital*

THE GOTHIC ANCESTOR OF THE WINDSOR CHAIR

192

Illustration 74   *—Robert C. Eldred*

A PRIMITIVE WINDSOR MADE IN WALES

This stick chair in its design is essentially a low-back Windsor combined with a very low comb-back. Presumably it dates from early in the eighteenth century. Beech and elm were the woods used.

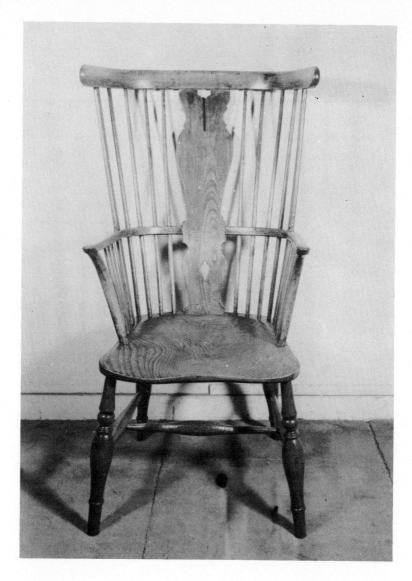

Illustration 75   *—Ashley Kent, Ltd.*

ENGLISH COMB-BACK WINDSOR WITH SOLID SPLAT

Its turned legs indicate that it was made by a provincial craftsman of the eighteenth century.

194

Illustration 76   *—Ashley Kent, Ltd.*

ENGLISH EIGHTEENTH CENTURY
BOW-BACK WINDSOR

Made of ash and yew with elaborately pierced back splat and front cabriole legs this chair is of the kind made by some London cabinet-makers.

Illustration 77   *—Ashley Kent, Ltd.*

ENGLISH EIGHTEENTH CENTURY
FAN-BACK WINDSOR

Chairs with back splats pierced with designs like this or more elaborate are sometimes called Chippendale from the type of piercing of
the splats but Thomas Chippendale never made Windsor chairs.

196

Illustration 78   *—Ashley Kent, Ltd.*

ENGLISH TRIPLE SPLAT ARMCHAIR

Here spindles have been entirely replaced by three back splats. They have a combination of urn and baluster shaping. The legs are braced by a cow's horn and spur stretcher.

Illustration 79   *—Ashley Kent, Ltd.*

ENGLISH EIGHTEENTH CENTURY
WINDSOR SIDE CHAIR

A loop-back Windsor where triple pierced splats have replaced
spindles. Made of yew and ash.

198

Illustration 80   *—Henry Clay Antiques*

ENGLISH NINETEENTH CENTURY
BOW-BACK WINDSOR

Made of beech and elm it is typical of the chairs made in or near High Wycombe before making Windsors there became factory work.

199

Section VI

CHECK LIST OF
KNOWN WINDSOR CHAIRMAKERS

ALLING, David................Newark, New Jersey, ca. 1800–1855

Made both Windsor and Fancy chairs. Painting of David Alling house and shop by unknown artist about 1840 is in collection of the New Jersey Historical Society. Shop and home was on Broad street, foot of William street.

ALLWINE, Lawrence....................................Philadelphia, ca. 1786

Claimed that he made "the best Windsor Chairs, gilt, plain and variously ornamented, being painted with his own patent colors." Branded fan-back side chair illustrated by Hornor.

ASH, Thomas...................New York City, ca. 1770–1815

"Thomas Ash, Windsor Chair Maker, At the corner below St. Paul's Church in the Broad–Way Makes and sells all kinds Windsor Chairs, high and low backs, garden and settees ditto. As several hundred pounds have been sent out of this province for this article, he hopes the public will encourage the business as they can be had as cheap and good, if not superior to any imported: he has now by him, and intends keeping always a large quantity, so that merchants, masters of vessels, and others may be supplied upon the

Note: Illustrated by Hornor refers to *Blue Book, Pennsylvania Furniture* by William MacPherson Hornor, Jr., Philadelphia, 1935 and Gates Collection to the Windsor collection of Mrs. Burton N. Gates, Worcester, Mass.

shortest notice. N.B. Shop goods will be taken in pay." *New York Gazeteer*, 17, 1774.

ASH, Thomas_____New York City, ca. 1815

"Fancy and Windsor Chair Manufactory Thomas Ash No 33 John–Street, Having by the death of his father succeeded to the long established and well known manufactory of Fancy and Windsor Chairs, takes occasion to solicit, from the public continuation of the favors which have been so long and so liberally bestowed on his predecessor. . . . On hand, an assortment of Chairs, both Fancy and Windsor, of the newest fashions and suited for domestic use of the foreign market." *New-York Annual Advertiser*, 1815

ASH, Thomas and William_____New York City, ca. 1785

Presumably the sons of Gilbert Ash, cabinetmaker. A sample chair with each of the four legs turned differently bears this label: "Thomas and William Ash, No 27 John St. New York, Where Windsor settees and Garden Chairs are made in the Neatest Manner."

Also, in the *New York Packet* of March 3, 1785, this advertisement appeared:

"Thomas and William Ash, Windsor Chair Makers, No 17 John Street, Beg leave to return their sincere thanks to the Gentlemen of this city and state and particularly to the Captains of Vessels, for the many favors they have received and would by the continuance of their commands. They now have ready at the Ware-House a great number of very neat Chairs and Settees, some of which is very elegant, being stuffed in the seat and brass nailed, a mode peculiar to themselves and never before executed in America."

ASHTON, Thomas_____Philadelphia, ca. 1790

Branded his chairs "Ths Ashton." A branded rod-back side chair is illustrated by Hornor.

204

AUSTIN, Richard................................Salem, Mass., ca. 1775–1826

Made fan-back and bamboo-turned Windsor chairs.

BARNET, Sampson................................Delaware, ca. 1789

Windsor chair bearing his label exhibited in 1950.

BAYNE, Nathanial................................Philadelphia, ca. 1790

With shop on Front street was listed as a turner. Presumably made both chair parts and Windsor chairs.

BERTINE, James:...........New York City. Late eighteenth century

A fan-back side chair is extant, branded "J. Bertine N.York."

BIGGARD, John................................Charleston, S.C., ca. 1767

Came from Philadelphia and was primarily a turner. On March 23, 1767 he advertised in *South Carolina Gazette* that he had opened a shop on Queen street "where gentlemen may be supplied with Windsor and garden chairs, walking sticks and many other kinds of turnery ware as neatly finished and cheaper than can be imported."

BLOOM, Matthius...........New York City, working 1787–1793

A fan-back side chair branded "M.BLOOM N.YQRK" is in the Van Cortlandt Manor historic house.

BOWEN, William................................Philadelphia, ca. 1786–1797

1786 paid occupation tax as chair and cabinetmaker
1794 listed as Windsor chairmaker
1787 succeeded by sons George and Thomas

205

BROWN, Nathaniel................Savannah, Georgia, ca. 1777–1803

Came from Philadelphia.

BROWN, Nathaniel................................Litchfield, Conn., ca. 1797

Advertised, 1797 in *Litchfield Monitor*: "Windsor and fiddle-back chairs. Shop near John Mattrocks, just west of the center of town." Again that he made "Windsor, fiddleback, dining room, parlor, kitchen and children's chairs."

BRIENTNALL, John............................Philadelphia, died 1747

One of the earliest Windsor chair craftsmen working in Philadelphia. In 1752 his daughter, Elizabeth married Thomas Ackley, (see)

C B............Probably New England, late eighteenth century or

early nineteenth century. Identity of this chairmaker has not been established. Known only for one chair branded "C B" which is privately owned in Buzzards Bay, Mass.

CATE, H..New England, ca. 1770

Known only by a child's bow-back chair that is branded "H.Cate."

CHAPMAN, J..............Philadelphia, late eighteenth century

Loop-back side chair branded "I Chapman" illustrated by Hornor.

CLARK & PLUMB..........................Litchfield, Conn., 1797

Oliver Clark and Ebenezer Plumb Jr. advertised: "Have taken the shop lately occupied by Ozias Lewis in the main

South Street. . . . They make heart back Cherry Chairs from 7 to 9 dollars each and Windsor ditto from 8s to 15s."

In 1799 partnership was dissolved and Clark worked alone in same shop.

COVERT, Isaac_____Philadelphia, ca. 1778–1805

1772 apprenticed to Joseph Henzey (see)
1783 paid £30 occupation tax
1786 paid £25 occupation tax
1802 sold "one large green Windsor chair" for $1.33.

COWPERTHWAITE, John K.___New York City, ca. 1815–1835

"FANCY AND WINDSOR CHAIR STORE JOHN K. COWPERTHWAITE Informs his friends and the public, that he has on hand at his long established Factory No 4 CHATHAM-SQUARE Extending through to No 2 Catherine-street NEW YORK an elegant and large assortment of Curled Maple, Bronze and Painted Fancy Chairs, likewise an extensive assortment of Windsor Chairs, Settees &c. of the newest fashions and warranted well finished, which he offers for sale on the most reasonable and accommodating terms. All orders will be thankfully received and attended to with punctuality and despatch. A liberal allowance to shippers. N.B. Old Chairs repaired, painted and re-gilt." *New York Annual Advertiser*, 1815

Members of this family continued to operate furniture stores in New York and Brooklyn until 1930.

CUSTER, J._____Location not known. Late eighteenth century

Known only by a fan-back chair that is privately owned in Baltimore, Maryland.

DOAK, William_____Boston, Mass., ca. 1789

Shop was on Back street.

DE WITT, John_____New York City, 1786-1801

When Federal Hall was remodeled for use of the Federal Government, he made Windsor chairs for the Senate and Assembly rooms for which city paid him £29/14. Made set of Windsor chairs with upholstered seats for Killiam K. Van Rensselaer of Claverack, N.Y. Label on them reads: "JOHN DE WITT/Windsor Chair Maker/No 47, Water Street near Coenties Slip, New York." Also advertised: "JOHN DE WITT Windsor Chair Maker begs leave to inform his friends and public in general that he continues to carry on the above business in all its branches at No 47 Water-Street near Coenties-Slip, New York. Likewise Garden Settees made in the neatest manner. Masters of Vessels may be supplied with either of the above articles in large or small quantities, at shortest notice. Punctuallity may be depended on." *Merchantile Diary and Advertiser*, Jan. 22, 1798

EDWARDS, Benjamin_____Northampton, Mass., ca. 1800

EVANS, Ephraim_____ Alexandria, Va., ca. 1736

Advertised as Windsor chairmaker, "lately come from Philadelphia."

FOSTER, Jesse_____ Boston, Mass., ca. 1796

Both Windsor chair and cabinetmaker.

FRENCH, John 2nd_____New London, Conn.

In 1807 he advertised in the *Connecticut Gazette*, "Windsor Chairs of all qualities and fashions made in the neatest manner for sale by John French 2nd."

FREEMAN & HOUCK_____ Philadelphia, ca. 1784

Was brief partnership of Benjamin Freeman and Andrew Houck. With shop on Front street between Arch and Race,

208

they made Windsors and rush bottom chairs. Both men apparently also worked separately.

GALER, Adam_____New York City, ca. 1774

"Adam Galer, Windsor Chair-Maker (lately from Philadelphia) in Little Queen Street next to the corner of Great George Street, opposite Hull's tavern, Makes and sells all kinds of Windsor Chairs. Any gentleman or masters of vessels may be supplied with a neat assortment upon reasonable terms." *New York Gazette*, Sept. 2, 1774

GAUTIER, Andrew_____New York City, ca. 1760–1767

First Windsor chairmaker to illustrate his advertising. A woodcut of a comb-back armchair with blunt-arrow legs.

"To be Sold by ANDREW GAUTIER in Princess-Street Opposite Mr. David Provost's near Broad-Street. A large and neat assortment of Windsor Chairs, made in the best and neatest Manner, and well painted, VIZ. High back'd, low back's Sackback's Chairs and Settees or double seated fit for Piazza or Gardens. . . . Children's dining and low Chairs &c.

N.B. As the above GAUTIER intends constantly to keep a large Number of all Sorts of the above Chairs by him for Sale, all Persons wanting such, may depend on being supplied with any Quantity, Wholesale or Retail, at reasonable rates." *New York Gazette*, April 18, 1765

GAW, Gilbert_____Philadelphia, ca. 1790

Shop was at 90 North Front street. His label reads:
"All kinds of/Windsor Chairs and Settees/Made and Sold by/GILBERT GAW/No. 90 North Front Street, twelve doors above Mulberry and Arch St./Where Merchants, Masters of Vessels and others/may be supplied at the shortest notice, at the/current prices for cash or approved notes.

N.B. Orders for the West Indies or any part of/the continent will be punctually attended to."

GAW, Gilbert and Robert_____Philadelphia, ca. 1796

On May 14, 1796, Washington bought 24 "oval back chairs" for $44.00 and on May 17, three more for $4.00. These were all shipped to Mount Vernon.

GILBERT, James_____Windham, Conn., ca. 1770

GILBERT, John_____Philadelphia, ca. 1783

GILPIN, Thomas_____Philadelphia, ca. 1770

It is recorded that he supplied twelve Windsor chairs for the Pennsylvania Hospital.

GOODRICH, Ansel_____Northampton, Mass., ca. 1795–1803

A labeled bow-back and a labeled fan-back were illustrated in *Antiques*, July, 1930. Advertised in *Hampshire Gazette*, "Ansel Goodrich Has on Hand and keeps constantly for sale a quantity of warranted Chairs, a few rods North of the Court-House, Northampton."

GORDON, John H._____Baltimore, Md., ca. 1833

His Windsor chair shop was at 41 Water Street.

GREEN, B._____Probably Connecticut, late eighteenth century

Known only from several chairs branded B. Green which have been found in different sections of Connecticut.

HALL, Richard_____Halifax, N.C., working 1770

Made set of eight fan-back side chairs for Royal White Hart Masonic Lodge No. 2, Halifax, N.C. that are still owned and used by this lodge.

210

HARRIS, William, Jr._____New London, Conn., ca. 1788

HARRISON, William_____Wilmington, Del., 1814

Listed in *Porter's Register* as Windsor chairmaker at 46 King Street.

HARDWICK, James_____Lexington, Ky., ca. 1794

"Makes Windsor chairs next door to Mr. White's the coppersmith." *Kentucky Gazette*, March 4, 1794.

HAYWARD, Thomas Cotton_____Charlestown, Mass., ca. 1800

Branded his chairs "T.C.Hayward".

HENZEY, Joseph_____Philadelphia, ca. 1770

Two signed fan-back chairs were on loan exhibition, Philadelphia, May 17, 1952 at meeting of the Society of Descendants of the Signers. His apprentices included Isaac Covert and David Stackhouse. (see)

HEWS, Alpheus_____New Haven, Conn., ca. 1787

"Alpheus Hews, from New Jersey, begs leave to inform his friends and the public that he carries on the business of Windsor Chair Making in Chapel Street, New Haven, where may be had any number of Windsor settees and Garden Chairs made in the neatest manner and different fashions, also some very convenient for children." *New Haven Gazette and Connecticut Magazine*, Feb. 22, 1787

HOLMES, Isaac_____Lexington and Frankfort, Ky., 1808

Advertised that he "has commenced business on High St." *Western World*, March 3, 1808

HUMESTON, Jay_____Charleston, S.C., 1802

Listed as Windsor chairmaker in 1802 directory.

HUMESTON & STAFFORD_____Charleston, S.C., 1798

"Humiston & Stafford, Chair Makers, Warranted Windsor Chairs and Green Settees, Of the newest fashion, and of an excellent quality, superior to any imported into this city." *Charleston City Gazette and Advertiser*, Nov. 28, 1798

HUMPHREYS, A._____Warren, R.I., 1824

"Cabinet Furniture and Windsor Chairs. The subscriber, respectfully informs the public that he continues to manufacture Cabinet Furniture of every description at his shop, opposite Capt. Nathan Child's Store." *Clarion of Bristol County Advertiser*, Jan. 10, 1824. Continued for many months.

HURDLE, Levi_____ Alexandria, Va., 1835

Announced that he had taken his brother Thomas I. Hurdle into partnership. "Will continue at the old stand, south-west corner of King and Columbus Streets, to carry on their business as Chair Manufacturers & Ornamental Painters, and where they will make, and keep constantly for sale at fair prices, a general assortment of Grecian, Fancy and Windsor Chairs." *Alexandria Gazette*, Jan. 1, 1835

JACQUES, Richard_____ New Brunswick, N.J., ca. 1750

Was "Spinning Wheel and Windsor Chair Maker."

KELSO, John_____New York City, ca. 1774

"John Kelso, Windsor Chair-Maker, from Philadelphia, at Mr. Hyer's in Broad-Street next door to the General's Makes and sells all kinds of Windsor chairs on the most reasonable terms and as he served a regular apprenticeship in one of the first shops in that way in Philadelphia, he is persuaded he can supply those who may be kind enough to favour him with their custom, with as well-finish'd strong and neat work as ever appeared in this city." *New York Gazette and Weekly Mercury*, Aug. 8, 1774

KUNTZ, Michael................................Philadelphia, ca. 1778

Made settees for refurnishing Independence Hall.

LAMBERT, John................................Philadelphia, ca. 1783–1793

Made Windsors in at least nine patterns, also serpentine back settees and children's chairs.

LAWRENCE, Daniel................................ Providence, R.I., 1787

"Daniel Lawrence informs the respectable citizens that he carries on the chair-making Business in Westminster street where he makes and sells all kinds of Windsor Chairs, such as Round About Chairs, Dining Chairs, Garden-Chairs, also sofas, settees, etc. in the best fashions, neat, elegant and strong, beautifully painted after the Philadelphia mode, warranted of good seasoned Materials, so firmly put together as not to deceive the Purchaser by an untimely coming to pieces."

LETCHWORTH, John................Philadelphia, ca. 1790–1805

One of the most prolific and successful Windsor craftsmen of Philadelphia. Made at least eight distinct types of Windsors. Mahogany arms left unpainted a feature of his work. In 1791 made chairs for the new City Hall, Fifth and Market streets. Made two sets of "Oval Windsor Chairs" for William Meredith in 1796, one painted green, the other white. Hornor illustrates at least two marked chairs. *Antiques*, January, 1951 illustrated a pair of marked Windsor love seats with mahogany arms.

LEIGH, John E. ....Trenton, N.J., ca. 1800

Labeled writing Windsor in loan exhibition at New Jersey State Museum, Trenton, in 1953. Label reads: "John E. Leigh, Cabinetmaker, 107 Factory Street, Trenton, N.J."

LOVE, B. .... Philadelphia, late eighteenth century

Branded loop-back side chair illustrated by Hornor.

MANNING, Caleb .... Salem, Mass., ca. 1800–1810

Before 1803 was in partnership with Samuel Harris, on Federal street 1805 was on Fish street near Gray's Wharf where he did cabinet work and made Windsor chairs.

MARSH, Charles .... New York City, ca. 1800

Made chairs with bamboo turnings. His label reads: "Charles Marsh, Windsor Chair Maker of 75 John St., New York."

MARTIN, Jacob .... Philadelphia, before 1791

His shop was on Front street.

MASON, John .... Philadelphia, late eighteenth century

Branded loop-back armchair illustrated by Hornor.

214

MATTOCKS, John_____Litchfield, Conn.

In 1797 advertised he would take in exchange "Basswood Plank proper for chair seats."

MACBRIDE, William_____New York City, ca. 1815–1825

Branded his chairs "W MACBRIDE N – YORK."

McKIM, Robert_____Richmond, Va., 1819

Listed as chairmaker in 1819 directory. Loop-back side chair bears label reading: "Robert McKim, Windsor Chair Maker, Post office, Richmond."

METCALF, Luther_____Medway, Mass., 1778–1838

"Wanted to Hire – – A journey man Windsor Chair Maker – also one or two active boys not exceeding 16 years of Age as apprentices to the Cabinet and Chairmaking Business." *Columbia Mercury*, April 14, 1801

NOBLE, Mathew_____Chatham, Conn., 1797

"Chairs of all kinds (except cabinet) made and sold by the subscriber, and new seats furnished to old chairs offered. He has a few sets common ones on hand and wants to purchase White Wood or Bass Plank, 18 inches wide and 2 inches thick." *Connecticut Courant*, March 27, 1797

ORMSBY, Orrin_____Windham, Conn., 1785

PARSONS, Theodosius_____Windham, Conn., 1792

"Wanted immediately a journeyman that is a good workman at the Windsor Chair and Cabinet business—to such an one good wages in cash will be given by applying to Theodosius Parsons, Windham (Scotland Parish)." *Connecticut Gazette*, Oct. 18, 1792

PINKERTON, John................................Philadelphia, ca. 1779

Made two settees for the court room at Independence Hall, also two settees for Pennsylvania House of Representatives.

POINTER & CHILDRES.................... Richmond, Va., 1782

Pointer is listed in Richmond, census of 1782. Known for a labeled Windsor chair.

REDMOND, Andrew.................Charleston, S.C., ca. 1774–1791

"Andrew Redmond still carries on at No 27 Meeting-street near the New Church at corner of St. Michael's Alley Turnery in all its branches. All kinds of House, Cabinet and Ship-Joiner's Work, Jobbing ditto etc. Likewise Philadelphia Windsor Chairs, either armed or unarmed, as neat as any imported, and much better stuff, etc." *South Carolina Gazette and General Advertiser*, Jan. 13, 1784

RICHARDSON, Elisha.................Franklin, Mass., ca. 1743–1798

Branded chair in Gates collection. Luther Metcalf (see) apprenticed to him, 1770–1778.

RICHMOND .... Philadelphia, 1763

Was an early Philadelphia maker of Windsor chairs. Shop was on Arch street. Probable maker of Windsor chairs for Carpenter's Hall.

216

RUSSELL, William, Jr.................New Bedford, Mass., ca. 1800

Loop-back chair with label reading: "Warrented/CHAIRS/ MADE and SOLD by WILLIAM RUSSELL, jun/Union Street NEW BEDFORD/MASSACHUSETTS" illustrated in *American Collector*, Sept. 6, 1934

SAGE, Lewis S.....................Northampton, Mass., ca. 1793

Both a cabinet and Windsor chair maker. "Desks, cases of drawers, tables bureas, frame chairs, Windsor chairs, plain do & other articles." *Hampshire Gazette*, Mar. 17, 1793

SCOTT, Edward.......................Boston, Mass., ca. 1801

Listed as Windsor chairmaker in 1801 directory.

SEAVER, William....................Boston, Mass., 1796

SEAVER & FROST.......................Boston, 1798

Hooded Windsor cradle bears this label: "WARRANTED/ WINDSOR CHAIRS/and Settees/In the newest stile, and of Superior Quality/Made and sold by SEAVER & FROST/Sign of the WINDSOR CHAIR/No 57 . . . . Street Boston./That no person may doubt the quality of said Chairs they offer that should their quality/not answer the expectations of the purchaser. to/return money provided complaint is made in reasonable time/. N.B. . . . Persons may be supplied on the shortest notice/Old chairs repaired and painted."

SHERALD, Josiah....................Philadelphia, ca. 1760

Made both Windsors and rush bottom chairs. "Made and sold by Josiah Sherald, at the Sign of the Gold-headed Cane in Second-street, a little below Dock Bridge, All Sorts of Rush-bottom Chairs, Windsor Chairs. Coches & C made in the best Manner, and newest Fashions, which he will sell low for Cash or short Credit. The said Sherald will barter Chairs for Goods at Cash Price." *Pennsylvania Gazette*, Sept. 5, 1765

SIMMS, Isaac......Probably Massachusetts. Late eighteenth century

Loop-back side chair in Gates collection is branded "Isaac P. Simms."

SMALL, Isaac..................................Newport, R.I., 1803

Listed as Windsor chair maker on Marlborough Street, near Friends Meeting House.

SNOWDEN, Jedidiah..................Philadelphia, ca. 1773–1786

Advertised as "Cabinet and Windsor Chair Maker" in 1773. Member, the Library Company in 1748 and 1749. Paid £100 occupation tax in 1786.

STACKHOUSE, David..................Philadelphia, ca. 1775

Was apprenticed to Joseph Henzey in 1772.

STACKHOUSE, Stacy..................Hartford, Conn., 1786–1795

"Stacy Stackhouse, from New York has established his business in this city where he makes and sells all sorts of Windsor Chairs in the neatest manner." *Connecticut Courant*, Jan. 30, 1786.

"Stacy Stackhouse Informs the public that he continues to make Windsor Chairs in the best manner, at his house a little

218

north of the State House in Hartford. Those Ladies and Gentlemen who will please to favor him with their custom, may depend of having their work done in the genteelest manner, and on as reasonable terms for pay in hand as in New York. Wanted by said Stackhouse, one or two likely lads, 14 or 15 years old, as apprentices to the above business." *American Mercury*, Oct. 8, 1792. Was succeeded in 1795 by John Wadsworth.

STAFFORD, Theodore_____Charleston, S.C., 1801

Had been partner of Jay Humiston. (See Humiston & Stafford) Directory of 1801 lists him as working alone at 98 Tradd. Not in 1802 Directory.

STEEL, Anthony_____Philadelphia. Late eighteenth century

Branded rod-back armchair illustrated by Hornor.

STONE, Ebenezer_____Boston, Mass., 1787

Advertised as Windsor chair and cabinetmaker, 1787 in *Massachusetts Gazette*.

TAYLOR & KING_____Philadelphia, ca. 1800

Were successors to John B. Ackley (see). Had shop on Front street. Chair and label illustrated by Hornor. It reads: "TABLOR & KING/Fancy & Windsor Chair Makers/Beg to inform their Friends and the Public that/they are now located . . . . . No. 1 to No. 5 Front St. be/tween Arch Street & high at the place formerly occupied by John B. Ackley where they intend to carry on their busi-/ness in all its various branches in the neatest manner and on/the best terms.

"Orders from Captains of Vessels and others for settees, chairs . . . anything/in their line will be thankfully received and punctually attended to.   PHILADELPHIA"

TAYLOR, Robert_____Philadelphia, after 1800

Made rod-back armchairs with mahogany arms for directors' room at Stephen Girard's bank. One illustrated by Hornor with label reads: "Windsor, Fancy Chairs and Settees/ ROBERT TAYLOR/Windsor & Fancy Chair Maker/Informs his friends and the Public that he continues to carry on the Windsor—and Fancy Chair making business in all its various branches and upon the most reasonable terms/at No 99 South Front Street (Near Walnut Street/where he has constantly on hand the most fashionable plain gilt and . . . chairs/

"Orders from masters of vessels and others who may favor him with their/custom shall be attended to with accuracy and dispatch."

TRACY, Ebenezer_____ Lisbon, Conn., 1744–1803

Known as Col. Tracy for his service in the American Revolution, he is the best known Connecticut Windsor chairmaker. Also has an extensive cabinetmaking business. Branded his chairs "EB TRACY." Examples in Garvan Collection, Yale Gallery of Fine Arts and Henry Ford Museum, Dearborn, Michigan.

TRACY, Elisha_____Scotland, Conn., 1743–1809

A cousin of Col. Ebenezer Tracy. Branded his chairs "E. Tracy." Branded chair in Gates collection.

TRUMBLE, Francis_____Philadelphia, ca. 1716–1798

Working by 1740, Shop was on Front street near Pine. Listed as Windsor Chair Maker in first Philadelphia Directory,

220

1785. According to the Cash Book of the Pennsylvania Assembly, payment was made to him on May 31, 1776, for 2 tables and 12 chairs. In August and November, 1778 he was paid £64/8/6 and £84/15/0 for round top armchairs, ditto plain, ditto low back and sack back Windsors. Bow back armchair, branded "F T" now in Independence Hall collection. Another branded "F. Trumble" has been exhibited.

TUCK, Samuel J.————————————————Boston, Mass., ca. 1795

Listed as Windsor Chair maker on Batterymarch street in 1795.

TUTTLE, James C.————————————Salem, Mass., ca. 1796–1849

Branded his chairs, "J. C. Tuttle." Branded side chair in Gates collection. Had shop first on Federal street "on the corner adjoining Boston Road" and later between Essex and Federal streets.

WADSWORTH, John————————Hartford, Conn., 1795–ca. 1810

Took over shop of Stacy Stackhouse. Advertised: "Windsor Chairs JOHN WADSWORTH INFORMS the public that he has taken the shop lately occupied by Stacy Stackhouse where he carries on the Windsor Chair-Making business: Those who will be pleased to employ him, may depend on having their work done in the best Manner, on reasonable terms and at the time agreed on:—Wanted by said Wadsworth, as Apprentices to the above business, one or two likely Boys, 13 or 14 years old:—Also to purchase a quantity of square edged Whitewood plank, from 18 to 20 inches wide." *Connecticut Courant*, Dec. 21, 1795

WALL, Richard————————————Philadelphia, ca. 1797–1820

Branded loop-back armchair illustrated by Hornor.

WEATHERSFIELD WINDSOR MANUFACTORY,
Weathersfield, Vt., ca. 1820–1830

Rod-back high chair bearing this label is privately owned.

WELLS, John I.————————Hartford, Conn., ca. 1798–1815

"John I. Wells Wants an apprentice to the Cabinet Making business. He has as usual Cabinet Furniture for sale, likewise Windsor Chamber and Kitchen Chairs of various kinds. He wishes also to sell a new Brass Clock, payment can be made easy. He wants to purchase scantling suitable for Bedstead and Cherry-tree boards; a little south of the Bridge." *Connecticut Courant*, Feb. 19, 1798

"John I Wells Continues the Cabinet & Chair making business at his shop south of the bridge Hartford." *Connecticut Courant*, April 12, 1812

WELLS & FLINT————————Hartford, Conn., 1806–1812

"John I Wells, Erastus Flint. The subscribers inform their friends and the public, that they have formed a connection in business under the name of Wells and Flint. Their business in the future will be continued at their former stand in Main Street." *Connecticut Courant*, April 12, 1812

The same year they advertised "an elegant assortment of Gilt, Fancy Bamboo and Fanback chairs to be disposed of on accommodating terms."

"The copartnership of Wells & Flint is this day dissolved by mutual consent." *Connecticut Courant*, April 12, 1812

WEST, Thomas————————New London, Conn., ca. 1815–1828

Advertised Windsor chairs in *New London Gazette* on April 26, 1815; March 22, 1823; and Feb. 27, 1828.

222

WIDDIFIELD, William............................Philadelphia, ca. 1785

A Windsor chair and cabinetmaker. Shop was on Spruce street between Front and Second streets. Branded his chairs "W. WIDDIFIELD."

WIRE, John..Philadelphia, ca. 1790

Shop at 207 South Front street. In 1792 made Windsors for Governor John Penn's house at Lansdowne, Price £18/7/6.

YATES, J..New York City, ca. 1790

Known only by an arch-back chair branded "I-YATES" that is privately owned in New Canaan, Conn.

The INDEX *begins on page 8.*

ACKNOWLEDGMENTS

Writing this account of the Windsor chair would have been an impossible task, far beyond the author's knowledge, were it not for the encouragement and assistance over some years of many collectors, dealers and museums. For pertinent information and making photographs available, he is indebted to.

American Philosophical Society; Alfred Arnold; Ruth and Roger Bacon; Ethel Hall Bjerkoe; John Kenneth Byard; Henry Clay Antiques; Mary Rose Cody; Lillian Blankley Cogan; Dr. George P. Coopernail; Warren W. Creamer; The Henry F. Du Pont Winterthur Museum; Robert C. Eldred; The Henry Ford Museum and Greenfield Village; Avis and Rockwell Gardiner; Ginsburg & Levy, Inc.; Greenberg's Antiques; Winifred E. Harding; Historical Halifax, N.C., Restoration Association; Mildred and Herbert Kaufmann; Ashley Kent, Ltd.; Joe Kindig, Jr.; Richard L. Mills; The Mount Vernon Ladies' Association; Museum of Fine Arts, Boston; National Park Service, United States Department of the Interior; The New Jersey Historical Society; Harry Shaw Newman; James B. O'Conner; The Pennsylvania Historical Society; Philadelphia Museum of Art; Quincy Historical Society; Israel Sack, Inc.; Charlotte and Edgar Sittig; Leon F. S. Stark; David Stockwell; John S. Walton, Inc.; White Hart Masonic Lodge No. 2; Ignatius M. Wiese and Ray Wilkinson.